Rethinking Cultural Transfer and Transmission

Reflections and New Perspectives

Studies on Cultural Transfer
and Transmission
Volume 4

Series ISSN
1879-7350

Series editor
Petra Broomans
Faculty of Arts
University of Groningen
P.O. Box 716
NL-9700 AS Groningen
p.broomans@rug.nl
www.petrabroomans.net

Series publisher
Barkhuis
Zuurstukken 37
NL-9761 KP Eelde
info@barkhuis.nl
www.barkhuis.nl

Rethinking Cultural Transfer and Transmission

Reflections and New Perspectives

Edited by **Petra Broomans and Sandra van Voorst**

assistant editor **Karina Smits**

Barkhuis
Groningen
2012

Cover design and typesetting: ColtsfootMedia, Nynke Tiekstra, Noordwolde
Book design: Barkhuis & Nynke Tiekstra

ISBN 9789491431197

For information about the series see 'About the Studies on Cultural Transfer and Transmission series', at the back of this volume

This publication was supported by a grant from the Netherlands Organisation for Scientific Research (NWO)

Table of Contents

Preface

The present volume, *Rethinking Cultural Transfer and Transmission. Reflections and New Perspectives*, is the last publication associated with the project 'Peripheral Autonomy? Longitudinal analyses of cultural transfer in the literary fields of small language communities', financed by the Netherlands Organisation for Scientific Research (NWO). The project began in 2006 and was one of the spin-offs of another project, 'Scandinavian literature in Europe: the influence of language politics, gender and aesthetics', itself part of the research programme 'Autonomy and the "new" Independence in the Arts'. Three universities have been involved in the project: Ghent, Groningen and Uppsala.

The first workshop, 'Reflection on Theoretical and Methodological Points of Departure', was held in Ghent in December 2006, with selected papers from the workshop published on the project's website. In December 2007, the second workshop, 'The Development of Literary Fields and the Influence of Foreign Literature from the Late Nineteenth Century until 1950', was held in Groningen, with selected papers published in the volume *In the Vanguard of Cultural Transfer. Cultural Transmitters and Authors in Peripheral Literary Fields* (2010), edited by Petra Broomans and Marta Ronne. In December 2008, the third workshop, 'The Invasion of Books. The Influence of Foreign Literature on Small Language Communities 1950 – Present Day', was held in Uppsala. Selected papers from this workshop were published in *The Invasion of Books in Peripheral Literary Fields. Transmitting Preferences and Images in Media, Networks and Translation* (2011), edited by Petra Broomans and Ester Jiresch.

In November 2010, a closing conference was organised in Groningen. At this conference invited speakers and participants in the project discussed the outcomes of the project and formulated new directions, such as gender aspects of cultural transfer, the importance of cultural transfer for minority literatures, and approaches to writing a cultural transfer and transmission history. The essays in this volume, the fourth in the series Studies on Cultural Transfer and Transmission (CTaT), are based on contributions to this conference. A new forum, which was developed to function as a scholarly environment favourable to intellectual exchange concerning cultural transfer and transmission (www.soctat.org), was also launched at the conference.

We would like to thank all our colleagues who participated in this project. We are also grateful to our assistant editor, Karina Smits, who helped with the editing and preparation of the manuscript.

Petra Broomans and Sandra van Voorst

Introduction

« Petra Broomans and Sandra van Voorst »

The essays in this closing volume of the 'Peripheral Autonomy?' project constitute both a continuation of previous research, as well as a reflection on new perspectives and a rethinking of the subject under study – cultural transfer and transmission. The questions still to be addressed include Which phenomena might be researched in the future and which fields? and Who are the actors in the fields and to what extent are their actions based on strategies or occur randomly? On the theoretical and methodological levels there are also questions to be posed. Do we have to contextualise or carry out textual analyses, such as content analysis? How does this research differ from translation studies? Can we use imagology? and Do we have to include book history and studies on materiality?

The study of cultural transfer and transmission is a relatively new research line within the broader context of literary history and cultural studies. After the pessimism expressed by scholars such as David Perkins in *Is Literary History Possible?* (1992) concerning the possibility of writing national or international literary history and the validity of the discourse of literary history, a revival of interest in national canons occurred at the beginning of the twenty-first century. Lively debates concerning what and who should be included in the canon were held, for example in the Netherlands and Denmark. At the same time, Peter Burke and Michel Espagne, *inter alia*, called for a transnational approach and greater focus on mediators within cultural studies, especially cultural transfer studies.[1]

1 Peter Burke, *Lost (and Found) in Translation: A Cultural History of Translators and Translating in Early Modern Europe* (Wassenaar, 2005); Michel Espagne, 'Jenseits der Komparatistik. Zur Methode der Erforschung von Kulturtransfers', in: Ulrich Mölk and Susanne Friede, eds., *Europäische Kulturzeitschriften um 1900 als Medien transnationaler und transdisziplinärer Wahrnehmung* (Abhandlungen der Akademie der Wissenschaften zu Göttingen, Philologisch-Historische Klasse, Dritte Folge, Bd. 273) (Göttingen, 2006), pp. 13-32. See also Petra Broomans, 'Zichtbaar in de canon. Spelregels voor cultuurbemiddelaars', *Tijdschrift voor Nederlandse Taal- en Letterkunde* 128 (3-4) (2012, forthcoming).

In the 'Peripheral Autonomy?' project we worked along lines based on these points of departure. Furthermore, we worked with the concept of 'cultural transmitter' rather than the limited term 'translator', and paid special attention to women cultural transmitters and minorities. We took our theoretical and methodological tools from Pierre Bourdieu and various interpretations of his concepts, including a feminist approach, and also used network analysis, cultural transfer and transmission studies and imagology (for a more elaborate overview see the contribution by Broomans and Ronne in this volume). The present volume highlights these new directions.

The first contribution to this volume is that by **Bo G. Ekelund**, 'The Citational Universe of Swedish Literary Scholarship: Transmitting and Reproducing an Unequal World in the Periphery', which is a good example of research in a field that is not immediately connected to cultural transfer and transmission studies. The chapter deals with the academic field, in which notions of centre and periphery are of importance. Ekelund's article charts the particular perspective on literature that is revealed by the PhD dissertation bibliographies produced by 680 literary scholars in Sweden between 1980 and 2005. While typically focusing on national literature, literary scholarship constantly negotiates the relationships between the semiperipheral literary field and the core of world literary space. In this negotiation, mastery of the conceptions of literature produced in the core is essential for semiperipheral cultural transmitters. The 'citational universe' of Swedish literary scholarship is to a great extent non-Swedish, and it is increasingly dominated by the Anglo-American academy. Looking more closely at regional and gender distributions of citations to key critics and theorists, the chapter points to 'site effects' that challenge scholarly orthodoxy: both geographical sites (e.g. the capital, with its dense literary networks) and institutional sites (such as departments of English, in which feminist and female-authored criticism are particularly favoured).

Another new perspective comes to the fore in the chapter by **Coppélie Cocq** entitled 'Sámi Storytelling as a Survival Strategy'. Cocq discusses the role of narratives in communities with endangered languages, using the example of the Sámi from Scandinavia, and finds that storytelling gives expression to survival and revitalisation strategies, as illustrated in contemporary Sámi productions. This study examines the role of narratives and the narrative practices of endangered languages in the process of place-making and as a source of knowledge, based on the study of Sámi inreach and outreach initiatives. Storytelling has become an important tool in revitalisation efforts. It is not only a rich tool for language teaching and acquisition, but also for identity management by members of the indigenous community. Furthermore, storytelling constitutes an important and often unexploited source of knowledge. Thus, it represents a place of negotiation and empowerment. Cocq's contribution shows how important the transfer of knowledge of their own identity is for minorities. Research into the meaning of cultural transfer and transmission in this respect will be one of the new research lines within future studies on cultural transfer and transmission.

Another aspect that was studied within the 'Peripheral Autonomy?' project was the role of the cultural transmitter. In the previous volumes, several scholars presented new material on forgotten individual cultural transmitters and discussed their lives and work. One question that arises in this regard concerns how this material is to be presented in a translation history? The following two contributions respond to this question.

In his article 'Translation History: Between Micro- and Macro-narratives', **Cees Koster** takes a look at some of the problems of writing a history of translation, from a practical as well as a theoretical point of view. He discusses the relationship between historical micro- and macro-narratives and argues that one should find a balance between, on the one hand, macro-narrative contextualisation, which can deal with issues of broader scope and scale concerning the material and cultural context of translation and, on the other, micro-narratives, such as a case study of a single translator in his or her role of cultural mediator, or a specific single source text, source author or source culture. To conclude his article, Koster exemplifies the theoretical considerations of writing a history of translation by presenting the outline of a hypothetical case. Koster illustrates the methodological and practical choices that have to be made and shows how macro- and micro-narratives may contextualise each other, and how these perspectives cannot do without each other.

In his article 'Translations and Translators in Swedish Literary History', **Lars Kleberg** discusses the visibility or invisibility of translations and translators in Sweden. He demonstrates that despite the fact that Sweden is and has been a translating country, translation history is generally neglected in the Swedish context. He takes a closer look at a number of general histories of Swedish literature from different periods and makes some comparisons as well as offering some reflections. It becomes apparent that earlier textbooks were more open to the role of translations in the evolution of Swedish literature than their contemporary successors. Furthermore, prospects for a possible Swedish translation history are discussed against the background of recent examples from England and Finland. To conclude his article, Kleberg presents a Swedish Translators Lexicon, the *Svenskt översättarlexikon*, which is currently being developed at Södertörn University Library. It is a database of bio-bibliographical articles about Swedish and Finland-Swedish translators from the Middle Ages to the present. This database is intended to be the source for research and eventually the basis for a History of Translation in Swedish.

The next article offers much material with which a historiographer within the cultural transfer and transmission field has to deal. The effect of the transmitted texts has to be contextualised and after the description of the lives and works of the cultural transmitters, their networks also have to be investigated. In the chapter, 'The Reception of Scandinavian Literature in the Netherlands and Flanders, 1860-1940: Some Preliminary Reflections on the Role of Networks', **Els Biesemans** and **Godelieve Laureys** discuss the reception of Scandinavian literature around the turn of the nineteenth century. In the first part of the paper they describe the nineteenth-century European reception of Scandinavian literature, including the personal attempts by Scandinavian authors to reach a broader audience. In the second part, the focus shifts to the context of reception in the Dutch language area. After a general description of the picture presented in existing research, the lives of two specific literary figures, Constant Jacob Hansen (1833-1910) and Marie-Elisabeth Belpaire (1853-1948), are examined in more detail, revealing that the situation is more complex than previously suggested.

Belpaire and other women cultural transmitters are also discussed in the following contribution, 'Peripheral Autonomy/Mutual Sympathy? Women Translators in Flanders, 1870-1914', where **Liselotte Vandenbussche** discusses the various motives of women writers in Flanders who were active from the late nineteenth to the early twentieth century in choosing particular authors or works for translation. The article provides a sketch of the – relatively minor – importation of foreign literature by women translators in Flanders between 1870-1914, focusing on the various source literatures and different kinds of imports. Special focus is placed on the wide-ranging motives of women translators, whether it was to earn money, to spread ideas and influence the reading public, or consolidate or prefigure an existing or future literary repertoire. The overview is supplemented with some background information on the secondary and higher education of women in Flanders and other elements that played a role in the translation market.

The role women played and the question of gender within the whole project is discussed by **Petra Broomans** and **Marta Ronne** in 'Gendering Cultural Transfer and Transmission History'. Attention is paid to rediscovered material and the development of new insights into individual women translators in the contributions concerned in the project. Broomans and Ronne also summarise the theoretical and methodological tools used in the research on gender and cultural transfer and transmission. In many cases the Bourdieuian perspective was used, as described in the article by Heilbron and Sapiro, available on the internet forum,[2] as well as network analysis. The article concludes with a call for an active, effective, dynamic and polyvoiced cultural transfer and transmission history that is full of dynamic women.

Rethinking Cultural Transfer and Transmission. Reflections and New Perspectives ends with two research proposals by the young scholars Karina Smits and Ingeborg Kroon. **Karina Smits** presents a research proposal concerning lesbian magazines in '*Die Freundin* and Other Relationships: A Proposal for a Comparative Study of the Role of Lesbian Magazines within the Process of Cultural Transfer and Transmission'. In 'Multicultural Literature: Exotic or Mainstream? A Proposal for a Comparative Study of Swedish Multicultural Literature in Translation', **Ingeborg Kroon** describes the possibilities of research on the perception of migrant literature after the cultural transfer process.

The articles collected in this volume demonstrate that the field of cultural transfer and transmission is developing steadily and offers a variety of new possibilities for research. Furthermore, the discussion concerning the theoretical points of departure and the methods used, which has only just begun, is already providing us with interesting results and insights.

2 http//www.soctat.org.

The Citational Universe of Swedish Literary Scholarship

Transmitting and Reproducing an Unequal World in the Periphery

« Bo G. Ekelund »

These days, we have little choice but to talk about the world. The age of the discourse of globalisation has become, in a very brief space of time, the age of the disciplinary agenda of world literature. However, if we are bound to reach for such planetary horizons, unthinkable as they are, our reach must extend from within decidedly more local contexts. In order to speak about the world, we must be able to map specific social worlds, always implying particular perspectives. The conception of peripheral autonomy stands as a challenge in this regard, a challenge to study how a local particularity relates to the world. We could complicate this relation by reminding ourselves that the very word 'periphery' originally comes from a vision of the world as being enveloped by airy regions, peripheries. The many national and regional literary worlds may be seen to be aspiring to that kind of globally enveloping form. And thus any reflection on the autonomy of a peripheral domain of literary production or reproduction is inevitably bound to bring in the term 'world literature'.

Ten years ago, Franco Moretti helped set the current agenda for literary studies with his 'Conjectures on World Literature' by holding 'world literature' up as a *problem*, one that called for methodological innovation. A host of responses has followed. We now have, for better or worse, a new field of study.[1] Even so, world literature still remains a problem, and the approaches to it are heading in very different directions. Ranging from Moretti's strategy of 'distant reading' to a renewed focus on the particularity of texts, as in the 'thickening process' advocated by Wai-Chee Dimock,

1 As evidenced by conferences such as 'The Rise of World Literature: The First Congress of the World Literature Association' in Beijing, summer of 2011; or the ACLA conference theme 2011: 'World Literature/Comparative Literature'.

the study of world literature itself appears as a kind of problem to be approached with some wariness.[2] We can at least state that Moretti's initial theses still stand in need of theoretical refinement and, more urgently, empirical work. I take as the point of departure for this article, which will be very much concerned with the latter task, the empirical groundwork, the cue that Moretti chose to adopt from world-system theory in the article already cited: 'international capitalism is a system that is simultaneously one, and unequal: with a core, and a periphery (and a semiperiphery) that are bound together in a relationship of growing inequality'.[3]

Similarly, to the extent that we can talk about such a thing, the world literature system is one and unequal. Such inequality, however, is not a static constant property of the system. Furthermore, it has to be made and maintained. Even with the methodology of distant reading, this particular aspect – the active making and maintenance of this basic inequality – will not be addressed, since a study of the relationship between texts may well reveal inequalities, but not how they are made and sustained. To study that active dimension, the way that history is made by humans – although not on conditions that they themselves have freely chosen – we must study the agents that produce, reproduce or challenge that inequality. As the work within the Peripheral Autonomy project has shown, cultural transmitters constitute a key category of agency affecting the flows within the airy periphery.[4]

The particular agents I will be concerned with here are to some extent cultural transmitters, although we might not wish to single out many of them as worthy of individual study in that respect. What I will look at is the academic part of that larger apparatus by which authors and books of various origins become available for the social practices we call literature. Seen from this perspective, the actual production of the literary text, the writer writing it, is a small part of literature. Instead, the larger part of literary life is comprised of the symbolic production and reproduction of the literary text. In Sweden, the work of production and reproduction of literature that takes place in the academy in this regard is continuous with, rather than separate from, practical criticism: both activities involve cultural transmission. However, in

2 Wai-Chee Dimock, *Through Other Continents: American Literature Across Deep Time* (Princeton, 2008), p. 79.

3 Franco Moretti, 'Conjectures on World Literature', *New Left Review* 1 (2000), pp. 54-68.

4 See Petra Broomans and Marta Ronne, eds., *In the Vanguard of Cultural Transfer. Cultural Transmitters and Authors in Peripheral Literary Fields* (Groningen, 2010).

both cases, the agents within this field have – as in most nation states – a primary responsibility for the symbolic production of the *national* literature: in the present case, of Swedish authors and books. We can see this in the proportion of reviews given to Swedish books in relation to the proportion of published titles, and we can see it in the objects of study of literary scholars.[5]

Even so, the semblance of a predominant Swedishness is tempered by the network of references to non-Swedish literary authorities that is constantly called upon in order to place and define what is Swedish and what is literary in Swedish literature. That is, the agents operating within this unequal universe constantly negotiate the relationships between the semiperipheral national field (Sweden), the core (the US, the UK, France, Germany), other semiperipheral national fields, and peripheral locations of production (the latter often mediated by the core). Moreover, since a great part of the literature that circulates in Sweden is of foreign origin, this mastery of conceptions of literature that are produced by the core countries of the world literary space is more or less crucial for critics and scholars, depending on the nature of their critical and disciplinary investments.

Given this state of mediations, it becomes an important task to map out the patterns of choices made by Swedish scholars who set their sails in the flows of theoretical and critical goods. What I propose here is to study Swedish scholars' references to foreign critics as an example of a transmission that appears secondary but is in fact fundamental to the local world in which the production, the reproduction and the transmission of *the literary* is the goal.[6] These referential strategies anchor academic literary discourse while at the same time allowing for the recognition of the critics' or scholars' specific mastery, their ability to bridge the nationally delimited field and the centres and the key peripheries of world literary space.

With such a mapping, a number of questions are raised. When Swedish literary scholars contribute to the reproduction of literature, what are the

5 In a survey of reviews of literary works classified in the database *Artikelsök* ('Article Search') between 1980 and 2005, roughly 70 percent of the reviews dealt with Swedish books. In the same period, according to book business statistics, the Swedish share of original titles of literature comprised between 41 percent and 52 percent. The object of study of 45 percent of all PhD dissertations is one or several Swedish authors.

6 See Pierre Macherey's notes on 'A theory of literary reproduction' for an emphasis on the process in which writers and critics sustain this permanently re-evaluated corpus that we tend to think of in terms of works, in: *In a Materialist Way: Selected Essays* (London, 1998), p. 50.

patterns of their reliance on non-Swedish ideas and theories? Do they change over time? Seen from the perspective originally alluded to, just how do literary scholars participate in the maintenance of this unequal space?

In what follows, I will present some results from an analysis of the secondary sources listed in Swedish dissertations between 1980 and 2005.[7] For our corpus, we first used LIBRIS (the Swedish National Library online catalogue) to identify all PhD dissertations classified as dealing with literature published in Sweden during those 26 years.[8] We included all dissertations defended at departments of literature (*Litteraturvetenskap*, 319 dissertations), departments of traditional modern languages (English, Romance, Germanic, 269 dissertations), and at other departments such as history, history of ideas, history of religion, and theology as long as the central object of study was a literary work or authorship (92 dissertations).[9] On the basis of these parameters, we had a database of 680 PhD dissertation bibliographies, with a total number of references falling just short of 200,000 (194, 558).

While almost 25 percent of the references could be classified as primary sources, the bulk of the bibliographies, 75 percent or more, list

7 This work was undertaken within the project 'Transnational Investments in Higher Education', funded by the Swedish Research Council, to whom I hereby express my gratitude. Many thanks also to Alexander Ekelund, who, apart from delving deep into the case of Julia Kristeva's reception, did much of the hard work of scanning bibliographies; and to Mikael Börjesson, who led the project and provided invaluable assistance in the statistical processing of the data.

8 LIBRIS is not an entirely reliable source, but for a large-scale inquiry it is the only practical option, and what it lists can be taken to comprise what is, at any given moment, the practically existing state of affairs. For a careful assessment of the shortcomings of LIBRIS and other Swedish bibliographical tools, see Åsa Warnqvist, *Poesifloden: utgivningen av diktsamlingar i Sverige 1976-1995* (Uppsala, 2007).

9 After some deliberation we decided to exclude those that used other alphabets or otherwise went beyond our own capacity for deciphering and coding the bibliographic information (about 40 dissertations were not included because of this linguistic threshold, the most significant exclusion being 14 dissertations about Slavic literature, as well as 4 in Arabic, 4 Chinese, 5 Greek, 2 Hungarian, 4 Japanese and 5 Latin). We also omitted dissertations whose engagement with literature as literature was deemed marginal, but we have retained a number of dissertations defended at departments of theology, history of ideas and history, in which the literary object of study was central, as far as we could judge.

secondary sources. It is the choice of those secondary sources that will be mapped to display the reproduction, in this Swedish field of scholarship, of a particular state of dependence. Outside of bibliometrics, there is, it seems to me, a lack of reflection on the role of citations, of the significance of secondary sources. Certainly this is so within literary studies. There was, in the heyday of postmodern interventions, an interest in, and a questioning of the boundary between secondary and primary, between fiction and non-fiction, between literature and criticism, but it seems safe to say that it has had little effect on scholarly practice, at least if one takes this corpus as the material evidence.[10] In individual dissertations, the secondary and the primary may flow into one another, and a small handful even display a kind of refusal to have their citational universe classified in this way, but on the whole the bibliographies announce the distinction clearly enough, either explicitly, in the traditional form of a hierarchically arranged list of works cited, or by simple inference from what the abstracts or keywords trumpet as the primary object of study. It is telling, perhaps, that the only dissertation that entirely refused the reader the convention of the bibliography was Horace Engdahl's study of the romantic text.[11] In order to include it, we had to compile our own list of works cited from the footnotes, which documented sources in the customary fashion.

Whether the boundary between the primary sources and the critical resources is drawn as an overt act of classification or exists only as an implicit relation between the object studied and the resources called upon to help in that study, it is in the choice of the latter that scholars place themselves in the flows that make and maintain an unequal literary world. The 'secondariness' of these references to critics and theorists also signifies a sort of intellectual unconscious, the deep ocean on which the primary references are afloat. The metaphor may seem an unnecessary mystification, but as Paul Wouters notes after having surveyed the field of citation studies, one constant is the lament that there is no satisfactory theory of citing.[12] That is why a quantitative analysis of a huge number of references is illuminating: while each diver in this sea comes up with a different list of titles, they are all affected by particular currents.

10 See, for example, Geoffrey Hartmann, *Criticism in the Wilderness* (New Haven, 1980); or Jacques Derrida, *Positions* (Chicago, 1981).

11 Horace Engdahl, *Den romantiska texten: en essä i nio avsnitt* (Stockholm, 1986).

12 Paul Wouters, *The Citation Culture* (Diss. University of Amsterdam, 1999), p. 9.

Each individual scholar would like to think that each citation is motivated by their particular argument, but clearly other forces are at work as well, forces we are bound to misrecognise. The size of this intellectual unconscious has, if anything, increased over the period we studied. The average share of secondary sources has risen from around 75 percent to around 80 percent. This is certainly not a drastic change, but the tendency seems clear enough, and the implications are interesting.

Some objections should be faced squarely at this point. First of all, there are clearly questions concerning what is measured by these references. The number of secondary sources listed need not say very much about the extent to which the dissertation text focuses on the positions argued in those sources. We all know that a dozen or more items can be thrown into a footnote that makes short shrift of the entire history of some once central controversy. They will still make up a dozen posts in the bibliography. However, even so, an absolute and relative increase in secondary sources cannot be dismissed as an illusion: we know, too, that each reference represents a search, and a more or less careful judgment of its value. The decision to include a reference is a decision about what makes up the recognisable world; that is, the world of scholarly recognition.

More to the point for the question pursued here, those secondary sources are to a large extent made up of non-Swedish critics and scholars. Not surprisingly, perhaps, the citational universe of Swedish literary scholarship is to a great extent non-Swedish. Exact figures for that distribution in the entire corpus are not available, since that would have meant coding geographical origin or place of residence for the more than 50,000 individual critics we have listed. Instead, we have worked with the category that will henceforth be referred to as the 'frequently cited critics' (FCC, and, more visibly in the discussion, the 'frequently cited foreign critics', FCFC), which is to be understood as those individual names that appear five times or more in the corpus as a whole and in more than one dissertation.[13] However, random checks of the remainder show substantially the same distribution, and as the following figures indicate, it is an extremely skewed one.

13 The notion of an individual name here also covers the instances of multiple authors, so that Theodor Adorno and Max Horkheimer, the authors of *The Dialectic of Enlightenment*, are one individual, while Theodor Adorno alone, the author of *Minima Moralia*, is another.

As shown in Table 1, the 4,166 frequently cited critics comprise less than 10 percent of the individuals who are cited, with a slight majority of them foreign critics. If we look at the citations attributed to these critics, however, we obtain a different picture of the weight of the most common critical resources. Ten percent of the individual critics cited account for nearly half of all the references. There is nothing to surprise us here, I assume, but there is a question about how to interpret such a picture. I suggest that one might see in that half of the references that cite critics who appear only once or a couple of times in the entire corpus the particularity of each scholarly project, the historical promptings voiced by the literary work or authorship that is in focus. The other half, which cite a small number of familiar names, on the other hand, represents the agreement scholars share about their discipline and its leading lights, perhaps outlining one key aspect, or mode of manifestation, of what after Donald Pease we may call a 'field imaginary'.[14] The mapping of the citational universe that I am undertaking here could thus be seen as an aspect of that field imaginary. The first point to be made about it is that the Swedish scholarly imaginary is to a very large extent beholden to global flows of intellectual goods.

Table 1 Domestic and foreign frequently and infrequently cited critics in 680 Swedish PhD dissertations on literature, 1980-2005.

	Individual critics	Citations
Frequently cited foreign critics	2,283 (4.5%)	32,619 (22.3%)
Frequently cited domestic critics	1,883 (3.7%)	36,532 (24.9%)
Infrequently cited critics, all	46,303 (91.7%)	77,111 (52.7%)
Total	50,469 (100%)	146,262 (100%)

Considering the peripheral autonomy of Swedish scholarship, what is of particular interest then are the critical resources that are imported into the Swedish field in these dissertations. There was a slight increase in the share of the secondary sources which represents the frequently cited *foreign* critics (the FCFC) in the 1980s and 1990s. This modest increase was mostly the result of a growth in the core of the national discipline, the departments of literature. In the modern languages, there is a fluctuation, but no clear trend. On the whole, however, it is at least clear that the importance of

14 Donald Pease, 'New Americanists: Revisionist Interventions into the Canon', *Boundary* 2 (17) (1990), pp. 11-12.

the foreign luminaries is not waning. The difference between what James Sosnoski called 'Master critics' and the 'token professionals' is not at risk of being erased.[15]

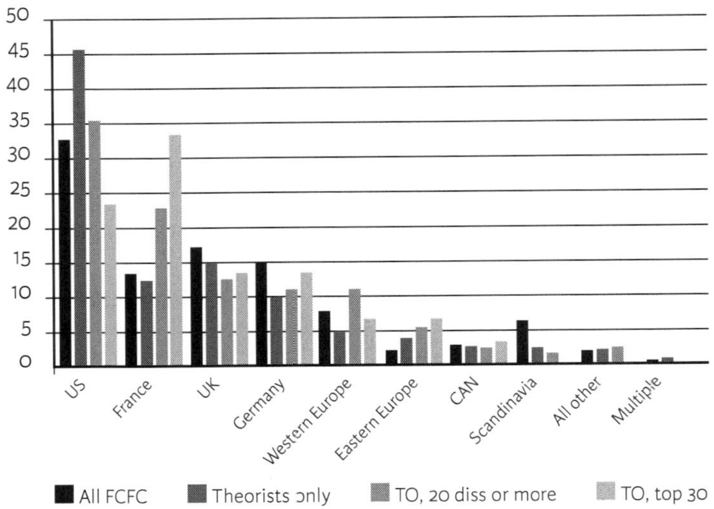

Fig. 1 Frequently cited foreign critics, by residence, percentages. "CAN" = Canada, Australia, New Zealand.

To sum up before we go on, there are clear indications that in the symbolic reproduction of 'literature' within the Swedish academy secondary sources are growing more important, and that within those secondary sources, the presence of foreign authorities has been increasing rather than decreasing. In other words, the academic production and reproduction of 'literature' has become more rather than less transnational in Sweden since 1980.

This transnational, non-domestic presence of frequently cited foreign critics amounts to 2,283 cited authorities. What sites of literary-critical production do they represent? Figure 1 presents the geographical location of the frequently cited foreign critics, by taking their main country of residence as an indicator. Choosing residence rather than origin, the figure accounts for the flows of intellectual migrants which is such an important feature of this world. As we can see, the black columns clearly point to the core of world literary

15 James Sosnoski, *Token Professionals and Master Critics: A Critique of Orthodoxy in Literary Studies* (Albany, 1994).

space: the US, UK, Germany and France. The US dominance is unmistakable, and if we focus on only those critics one may designate 'theorists' – the dark grey columns – this dominance is even greater.[16] However, if we look at the top of the pyramid, the relations shift. Counting only those theorists cited in at least 20 dissertations, the French column rises noticeably, and if we look at the top 30 theorists, by number of dissertations that cite them, we see that US dominance does not extend to this pinnacle. It is worth noting that of the seven top theorists that make up the light grey US column, only three were educated in the US. As we all expect, the apex of the secondary-sources pyramid is located in France, and at its very top we find Roland Barthes.

However, if French theory, in the form of Barthes, holds this preeminent spot, it does so after thorough mediation by that single and unequal system that we took as our starting point. Of the 367 citations to Roland Barthes in 170 dissertations, 213 cite works published outside France (36 percent published in English, 19 percent in Scandinavia). We are not making a point about the introduction of Barthes into Sweden here, but only emphasising the different types of access academic critics have had to the work of Barthes. Translation into English and Swedish is clearly crucial in this regard, when the single most common reference to Barthes is to a book entitled *Image Music Text.* Hats off to Stephen Heath, the translator and editor of that book.[17] With a figure like Heath, we are dealing with a kind of cultural transmitter who has become increasingly important in the postmodern period: almost equal prestige is now given to those who introduce and translate works of theory and intellectual speculation as to those whose work is devoted to literary authors. A paradigmatic case in this development is Gayatri Spivak's translation of *Of Grammatology*, which provides a flash portrait of the kind of coup that a successful translation and introduction of a major foreign theorist amounts to.[18]

16 Classification of the critics cited as theorists, literary historians, literary critics, etc., is a problematic exercise. For this rough identification of theorists we have firstly relied on the *Johns Hopkins Guide to Literary Theory & Criticism*: inclusion in it has been taken as sufficient grounds for identification. However, we added a number of names when we felt that similar criteria were fulfilled, e.g. the works cited develop conceptual issues or present models of general import rather than findings that relate to one empirical object; the critic is treated as belonging to a particular theoretical movement or school.

17 Roland Barthes, *Image-Music-Text*, translated by Stephen Heath (New York, 1977).

18 Jacques Derrida, *Of Grammatology*, translated by Gayatri Spivak (Baltimore, 1974).

The importance of this kind of mediation in the Swedish field of scholarship becomes even more obvious if we move to critics who did not write in English, French or German. Of all the citations to Mikhail Bakhtin in our material, 47 percent refer to Scandinavian publications and 36 percent to US publications.[19] As we see in this case, one of the great names of the wave of theory that broke over Sweden from the mid-1970s onwards, Bakhtin, becomes broadly available through translations into English and Swedish, and especially the essays translated as *The Dialogic Imagination* in 1981 (translated by Caryl Emerson and Michael Holquist, 62 citations) and *Det dialogiska ordet* (The Dialogic Word) in 1988 (translated by Johan Öberg, 67 citations).[20]

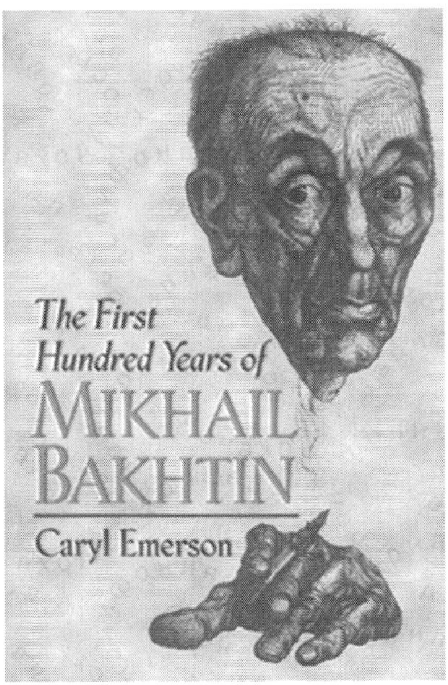

Caryl Emerson not only translates his work, she has also written several books on Mikhail Bakhtin.

19 Had we included dissertations from Slavic departments, we would no doubt have had a higher figure for the 'other' category.

20 Mikhail Bakhtin, *The Dialogic Imagination*, translated by Caryl Emerson and Michael Holquist (Austin, 1981); Mikhail Bakhtin, *Det dialogiska ordet*, translated by Johan Öberg (Stockholm, 1988).

The availability of Bakhtin's writing in either English or Swedish is a necessary condition for the broad use of his ideas in Swedish dissertations. Whether this is a sign of peripheral autonomy or heteronomy is a difficult question. The early uses of Bakhtin's ideas largely relied on American translations, as did Hans-Göran Ekman in 1975, the first Swedish PhD dissertation to cite Bakhtin.[21] However, it is worth noting that copious references to Bakhtin distinguish the core discipline of this field: it is in literature departments that Bakhtin becomes a particularly significant critical resource, more than in language departments.[22] The strong showing when it comes to translations into Swedish of Bakhtin is an index, perhaps, of the powerful appropriation of this Soviet thinker by the national pole of Swedish literary scholarship. However, in this matter we need comparative results in order to determine whether the appropriation obeys an internal dynamic or whether it reflects general movements in world literary space. Note also that despite the fact that Bakhtin's influence on Swedish scholarship is significantly connected to the reception of Julia Kristeva, very few scholars use the early French translations.[23]

The particular mediations that take place in the peripheral, or as I would have it in this case, the semi-peripheral context, do point us towards the importance of independent developments within a given national field. The basic measure of relative autonomy is to be found in the power of a given field to *translate* whatever is imported from outside into the terms of the field itself. In order to speak of a measure of peripheral autonomy with regard to the use of 'global theory' we would have to be able to point to particular deviations from more general patterns. While the comparative work that is needed in order to make such points is not yet present, we can still register some such particularities if we look at the mediation of the main French theorists as they enter this space.

21 Hans-Göran Ekman, *Humor, grotesk och pikaresk: studier i Lars Ahlins realism* (Staffanstorp, 1975). The claim of primacy made by Michael Gustavsson in 'Litteraturteorins expansion. Svenska doktorsavhandlingar i litteraturvetenskap 1976-1985', in: Bengt Landgren, ed., *Universitetsämne i brytningstider* (Uppsala, 2005), p. 549.

22 Reminding ourselves, of course, that the Slavic languages were not included in this analysis.

23 See the case study by Alexander Ekelund, *Julia Kristevas genomslag i Sverige – fransk feminism som symbolisk tillgång i litteraturkritikens fält* (Uppsala, 2011), p. 12.

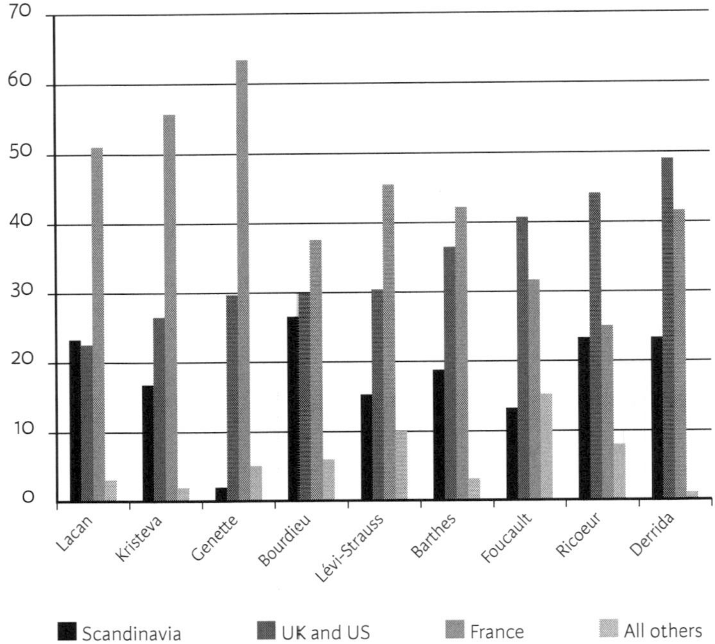

Fig. 2 French theorists cited in Swedish PhD dissertations in literature, by publication site, percentages.

Figure 2 shows places of publication, in proportions, for the most frequently cited French theorists. As we can see, the least mediated, or the most 'French' French theorists are Jacques Lacan, Julia Kristeva and Gérard Genette, while the most Anglo-American thinker from France is Jacques Derrida, with Paul Ricoeur and Michel Foucault following closely. Foucault is also interesting because he is the only French grand theorist who has a sizable chunk of citations referring to German-language sources. And the most Scandinavian French theorist is Pierre Bourdieu.

In terms of an autonomous scholarly practice, these differences are difficult to assess. Those scholars who have direct access to the original publications may be in a position to deal directly with the ideas in their particular, local context, and thus contribute directly to the reproduction of that theory. However, that would require gaining recognition for one's contribution in the original field of production. To have a theorist's ideas translated and discussed in one's own language, on the other hand, means that a relocation of the ideas has taken place, and the conditions for local, domestic development are at least theoretically in place. The results seem to support the argument that the particular mediation of Derrida is Atlantic rather than continental, at least if we take this space of scholarly production as a whole. No doubt there are great differences between the early transmission of Derrida's thought by the intellectuals associated with the journal *Kris*, on the one hand, and the large-scale use of Derrida in PhD dissertations in the late 1990s, on the other; the straightforward picture of a French thinker that is transmitted to Sweden via the US is false in this respect.[24] However, in terms of the larger availability of this critical resource for the work of reproduction, it is clear that the English translations are decisive. For Genette, Kristeva and Lacan, I think we likewise need different analyses for each case, and the same can be said of Bourdieu. The almost total absence of translations into Swedish of Genette is interesting and would seem to have to do with the fact that he is the most narrowly literary of these theorists; in fact, he is the only one of them who is a literary theorist properly speaking, and for that reason his work may have less appeal to the general Swedish book market. The first translation of Genette's work into English also came quite late, in 1980.

However, more importantly than such specific mechanisms may be the more institutional one that also corresponds to Bourdieu's thesis about position-takings and positions: the least mediated French theorists are also the ones associated with the core discipline and the capital. If one looks at the distribution of the citations to the top theorists in a geometric spirit, what is revealed is a striking overrepresentation of Stockholm University, especially for the least mediated theorists. Some figures that indicate the phenomenon I am pursuing: while the share of total citations represented by Stockholm University is 24 percent, its share of Kristeva citations is 40 percent, of Lacan and Genette 34 percent and 35 percent. Similarly overrepresented in Stockholm are Derrida and Foucault. Bourdieu is a different kettle of fish, with a very strong showing in Uppsala, but then Uppsala is the centre for the sociology of literature in Sweden.

24 The first issue of the journal *Kris* came out in December 1977, and its first editorial board included Horace Engdahl, Anders Olsson and Arne Melberg. *Kris* introduced the new theoretical discourse in articles that dealt with textuality, deconstruction and aesthetics. Direct translations of various continental thinkers helped cement the importance of *Kris* to both the academic and the general debate on literature. In 1980, Derrida sent 'La loi du genre' to *Kris*, and it was published for the first time in French and in a Swedish translation in the September issue.

What we can clearly see then, is a 'site effect', to use Bourdieu's term, the fusion of social and geographical space that proves a fertile ground for engagements with leading theorists. Whether that local focus on high French theory is a sign of autonomy or heteronomy is again a matter of how one poses the question. According to Pascale Casanova's analysis of world literary space, the most autonomous practices in the least autonomous parts of this global space are the ones that refuse national-political and market constraints.[25] Sweden's literary field, broadly understood, is perhaps not one of the *least* autonomous national fields, but it is very far from being a central one. Thus, what counts as autonomy within the local boundaries may stand in a very uneasy relation to literary autonomy globally understood. What does the overrepresentation of new French theory at Stockholm University thus signify? No doubt it has a great deal to do with the general cultural milieu of the capital and the kinds of network effects it enables. Editorial staff and writers at avant-garde periodicals such as *Kris* or *OEI* move in and out of the academy, and it is apparent that some of the most cutting conflicts over positions in the Swedish academy have reflected the poles of academic capital and avant-garde cultural capital.[26] What happens in such circumstances can best be understood as the defence of a *nationally* delimited autonomy of academic practices against a challenge that relies on avant-garde achievements that have not yet been successfully transmitted into the national field. It follows that from the viewpoint of established positions within the national field of academic production, the pretenders who engage in an open traffic with journalistic or essayistic criticism, importing various heterodox thinkers from the continent, should be rejected not least as representing heteronomous sectors, where the borders demarcating sound academic practice are porous against the tides and waves

25 Pascale Casanova, *The World Republic of Letters* (Cambridge, Mass., 2004), pp. 169-170.

26 See for example Hanne-Lore Andersson's summary of the debate over Aris Fioretos' dissertation when Fioretos applied for a post at Stockholm University in 1993, pp. 173-178.

of intellectual fashion.[27] By contrast, from the perspective of this intellectual avant-garde – which is in touch with what it sees as the international cutting edge of literary thought – those who patrol the borders of national academic orthodoxy are inevitably engaged in reargued actions against modernity (or postmodernity, as the case may have been).

When the dust settled after the early collective transmission of French theory into Swedish literary studies, Derrida, Barthes and Kristeva, among others, had become the common currency of literary discourse: a successful cultural transfer had been carried out.[28] According to Hanne-Lore Andersson, who has studied the debates within Swedish literary scholarship around the turn of the twenty-first century, new theories failed then – and had failed earlier – to disturb the doxa of this field, a doxa she defines as the primacy of textual analysis.[29] There is some truth to this, although our geometric analysis of the qualitative position-taking points in a slightly different direction than Andersson's study of the debates. What the cultural transmission of foreign theory into a peripheral field mainly serves to do is to challenge orthodoxy rather than doxa. It is also fuel for the mobilisation of particular constellations of scholars within new generations of actors.[30] As Andersson notes, feminist scholars were at the centre of many of the debates about the fundamental values of the field.[31] It seems more than likely that the mobilisation of theory on the part of female entrants into the field is of key importance in the period

27 While there is little that connects the two cases in substance, it is extraordinarily illuminating to think of this relationship between the established academic positions and the new theoretical imports made by the circle around *Kris* in the terms employed by Bourdieu to analyse Roland Barthes' challenge to the staid academic conservatism of the French 'literary state' from that 'point of least resistance to the field, where what is called fashion continually flowers' (xxi-xxii, *Homo Academicus*, English translation). Barthes, in Bourdieu's analysis, represents 'the peak of the class of essayists' and as such has a sensitivity to what is new and intellectually exciting that is entirely lacking within the core of the distinctly academic study of literature.

28 See Broomans and Ronne, *In the Vanguard of Cultural Transfer*, p. 7.

29 Hanne-Lore Andersson, *Doxa och debatt* (Gothenburg 2008), p. 194.

30 See Donald Broady and Mikael Palme, 'Inträdet. Om litteraturkritik som intellektuellt fält', in: Donald Broady, ed., *Kulturens fält* (Gothenburg, 1998), pp. 173-215.

31 Andersson, *Doxa*, p. 197.

studied. The citational universe of Swedish literary studies was and largely remains a male-dominated one, but this period saw concerted attempts to challenge that part of the orthodox formation of the discipline. A discussion of citations as a form of cultural transmission in this period cannot skirt the question of the gendering of citational practices. We will turn to this question below, with a look at the distribution of references to female and especially feminist foreign critics.

On the whole, there has been a fairly steady increase in the proportion of female (not necessarily feminist) critics among the frequently cited foreign critics across the entire period, albeit from very modest levels, as can be seen in Figure 3. The solid line plots the share of citations to female critics, while the dotted line represents the share of dissertations that were written by women. Both curves rise over this period, but there is no mechanical correlation between them. Moreover, it is clear that even when a dissertation is written by a woman, the share of citations to female critics among the frequently cited foreign critics is very low, never rising above a yearly average of 20 percent even in years when the female authors account for 66 percent of all dissertations.

Fig. 3 Share of female-authored dissertations among Swedish PhD dissertations in literature (left-hand axis) and share of citations to female critics among the frequently cited foreign critics (right-hand axis). Two-year intervals.

Table 2 **Share of citations to female critics and mean number of citations to feminist theorists according to discipline, in Swedish PhD dissertations.**

Discipline	Mean share of female critics among FCFC	Mean number of citations to feminist theorists among FCFC	N, diss.
Literature	15%	5,3	112
English	23%	8	87
French	11%	3,8	18
German	13%	2,7	16
Other	15%	5,9	35
Total	16%	6	268

Lacking comparative data, it is difficult to assess this slow increase in the presence of female critical resources in the Swedish field. One thing is clear: these levels would be even more modest were it not for the citation practices among English department PhDs. The mean share of female critics cited among the frequently cited foreign critics in these dissertations was 23 percent over the whole period, while in literature departments it was 15 percent, and it was even lower in all the other departments, as shown in Table 2. A similar pattern emerges if one looks only at citations of explicitly feminist theorists. Again, the figures for dissertations from English departments are significantly higher. One might jump to the conclusion that this is simply a reflection of the higher degree of feminisation of English literary studies than within the core discipline of literary studies in Sweden, but there is no such mechanical correlation. If one looks only at the female-authored dissertations, the citing pattern shows that feminist theory has a larger presence in departments of English: 68 percent of the female-authored dissertations from English departments cite foreign feminist theorists, while the corresponding figure for literature departments is 45 percent, and the French departments are the least feminist in these terms (28 percent).

These figures cannot directly be taken to prove that the scholarship itself is more feminist in English departments, but in the recognition of critical authorities measured by citations, the PhD scholars from English departments were more inclined to bring in female critics and feminist theorists than their counterparts in the core discipline of this field. Attempts to understand this, it seems to me, take us again to the paradoxes of local, nationally delimited autonomy in relation to global forces. Our overall analysis of these citation patterns shows an increasing US dominance among the foreign resources accessed by Swedish PhD students. The English departments, in this regard, are the most 'open' to that hegemonic influence, but at the same time, perhaps since they are the dominated within their national field, they are attuned to systems-critical resources such as feminist theory, postcolonial theory and theories of minority literatures, all of them richly available within the Anglo-American field of academic production. The national autonomy at the core of the Swedish field seems, by contrast, restricted to a more conservative range of recognised citational resources. Certainly, our analysis points towards a picture that confirms Andersson's claim that textualisation is the 'doxa par préference' of the literature departments, while English department PhD students are more oriented towards the contextualising tendency seen in some of the theoretical movements that emerged in the late 1980s and early 1990s.[32]

The Oxford English Dictionary tells us that the chief meaning of periphery these days is: 'the outlying areas of a region, most distant from or least influenced by some political, cultural, or economic centre'. It is interesting to note that this definition seems to include autonomy as a given for peripheral areas, or if not autonomy then at least a distance from the power at the centre. That distance is no doubt the greater the closer one comes to the national centre of an inherently conservative discipline such as literature. The citational universe of Swedish doctoral scholarship in literature shows that this peripheral autonomy includes strong internal tensions introduced by agents who, in different ways, open the door to the autonomous forces of intellectual work globally. In this way, they help to reproduce a particular state of dependency on the global centres of theoretical and critical capital, and thus contribute to the unequal distribution of that capital. Perhaps a solid knowledge of these patterns can at least allow for a constant self-reflexive questioning of that dependency.

32 Andersson, *Doxa*, p. 193.

Sámi Storytelling as a Survival Strategy

« Coppélie Cocq »

This article discusses the role of storytelling in communities with endangered languages, using the example of the Sámi from Scandinavia. The continuity of the Sámi storytelling tradition can be observed in the many adaptations of older sources to recent productions in children's books, media and on the internet. This continuity indicates the significance of this tradition but there are questions about the different meanings it is assigned in a contemporary context and about today's storytelling practices.

Here I will consider to what extent storytelling gives expression to survival and revitalisation strategies, that is, the efforts of a group to articulate cultural aspects and traditions they consider to be vital for their continued existence. These efforts will be approached through three recurrent elements of Sámi discourse about narratives: the role of storytelling (1) for endangered languages, (2) in the process of place-making and (3) as a source of knowledge, based on the study of Sámi inreach and outreach initiatives. My hope is to contribute to a discussion about the use of storytelling in the strengthening and revitalisation of minor languages.

In this study, storytelling is approached from a folkloristic perspective, that is, as an artistic form of communication[1] that is of significance to the social life of the community from which the stories emerge.[2] It is a vehicle for cultural and traditional knowledge, in other words, knowledge specific to a group or a community which is conveyed from generation to generation.[3] Legends, historical accounts and personal narratives are considered in relation to their context and to the social reality with which they interplay. Thus, this approach highlights how narration, as a central form of communication within a group, can convey strategies for cultural and linguistic revitalisation through new practices, efforts and purposes such as those that can be found today.

1 Dan Ben-Amos, 'Toward a Definition of Folklore in Context', *The Journal of American Folklore* 84 (331) (1971), pp. 3-15.

2 Richard Bauman, *Story, Performance and Event. Contextual Studies of Oral Narrative* (Cambridge, 1986).

3 Cf. Jonas Frykman and Orvar Löfgren, *Den kultiverade människan* (Lund, 1979), p. 48.

The use of storytelling to teach, promote and protect endangered languages is illustrated in many examples internationally. Adaptations of legends and tales to new media can be found, for example, in indigenous contexts in Australia and North America.[4] Innovative projects make use of film[5] or virtual environments[6] for the renewal of traditional stories. Not surprisingly, similar ongoing projects and initiatives can be found in Sápmi (Samiland).

The rich Sámi storytelling tradition is witness to its capacity to convey information, educate, socialise and entertain. Its role in the articulation of norms, values and discourses has been emphasised in previous research.[7] Written versions of traditional tales were published at the turn of the twentieth century, as early adaptations of an oral source to a book format. Numerous and increasing numbers of instances of Sámi storytelling can be found in various media today: short tales on television[8] and radio,[9] digital books[10] and numerous online productions. This study focuses on contemporary Sámi productions that refer explicitly to the oral traditions, for example, to sources gathered by lappologists and early Sámi authors. Motifs based on characters, topics and settings can be found in most collections of Sámi legends. The continuity of the storytelling tradition is in itself proof of its significance, although the variations in content and contextual premises should be taken into consideration.

4 For example, Brett Leavy, 'Digital songlines: Digitising the Arts, Culture and Heritage Landscape of Aboriginal Australia', in: Laurel Evelyn Dyson, Max Hendriks and Stephen Grant, eds., *Information Technology and Indigenous People* (Hershey, 2007), pp. 159-169; and 'The Conne River Project' at http://www.storiesofconneriver.ca/EN/about/index.php, accessed July 10, 2012.

5 Tales Productions, *Raven Tales* (2004), http://web.archive.org/web/20080622211621/http://www.animated-news.com/archives/00001550.html, accessed July 10, 2012.

6 'The Conne River project'.

7 E.g., Coppelie Cocq, *Revoicing Sámi Narratives. North Sámi Storytelling at the Turn of the 20th Century* (Umeå, 2008); Phebe Fjellström, *Samernas samhälle i tradition och nutid* (Stockholm, 1986).

8 Utbildningsradion, 'Små sagor', http://www.ur.se/Produkter/162789-Smasagor-sydsamiska?q=sydsamiska, accessed July 19, 2012.

9 SVT Sápmi, *Stállu ja garjá* (1997); SVT Sápmi, *Stálu čalbmi* (2002).

10 Elmira Zadissa and Ramona Zadissa, 'Kulturstorm *Gos lea Nora gielká?*', http://kulturstorm.se/barnbok/Davvisamegiella/noraspulka_davvisamegiella.html, accessed July 19, 2012.

The Sámi are the indigenous people of northern Europe, living in Norway, Sweden, Finland and Russia. Although we lack official figures, the Sámi population is estimated by the Swedish Sámi parliament to be about 80,000. There are about ten different Sámi languages, of which North Sámi is the most widely spoken.[11] The diversity of languages and livelihoods, as well as the division of the Sámi's homeland between four countries, have resulted in varied conditions for the people and their languages.

The status of minority languages in Nordic countries evolved in accordance with the general ideology regarding minorities that can be observed elsewhere in Europe. From the late nineteenth to the mid-twentieth century, stigmatisation and assimilation were common aspects of minority politics.[12] This ideology, made concrete in political measures discriminating against the Sámi, has left profound marks. Sámi ethnicity has been questioned, land rights jeopardised, and a great number of Sámi have grown up without learning the language of their parents. The Sámi languages are today endangered.[13]

During the last decades we have witnessed a drastic change in minority politics. Since the 1990s, the Sámi of Norway, Sweden and Finland have had their own parliament, while the ratification of the Framework Convention for the Protection of National Minorities and of the European Charter for Regional or Minority Languages by the three countries in the 1990s and early 2000s was a concrete new step in minority politics. The treaties aim to protect and promote historical regional and minority languages and for the first time articulate an effort to protect the Sámi languages and acknowledge the value of the languages spoken by the Sámi minority.

The recent changes in minority politics have implied new conditions, premises and possibilities for the minorities of Scandinavia. A process of revitalisation, that is, 'efforts to halt the process of language shift and to

---

11 Ulla-Maija Kulonen, Irja Seurujaärvi-Kari and Risto Pulkkinen, eds., *The Saami: a Cultural Encyclopaedia* (Helsinki, 2005); Mikael Vinka and Elisabeth Scheller, 'The Saami Languages', in: *The Barents Encyclopedia* (forthcoming).

12 Lennart Lundmark, *Stulet land: svensk makt på samisk mark* (Stockholm, 2008); Lars Elenius, *Nationalstat och minoritetspolitik. Samer och finskspråkiga minoriteter i ett jämförande nordiskt perspektiv* (Lund, 2006).

13 Cf. James Anaya, *The Situation of the Sami People in the Sápmi Region of Norway, Sweden and Finland. Report of the Special Rapporteur on the Situation of Human Rights and Fundamental Freedoms of Indigenous People* (2011).

promote the usage of a heritage language',[14] can be observed through the Sápmi region in varying degrees of intensity across the different groups. Revitalisation efforts are expressed through an increasing number of cultural events and initiatives promoting Sámi languages and culture and through the increasing support of media and politics.[15] Revitalisation is about the 'transmission and survival of Indigenous languages despite pressures to assimilate'.[16] Moreover, in the case of the Sámi, revitalisation also strives for the creation of new speakers by offering practices that facilitate language acquisition. Language endangerment is a serious matter, demanding that we investigate every strategy that might contribute to the survival and revitalisation of languages. From this perspective, I propose to approach storytelling as an indigenous strategy for the transmission and survival of languages.

Storytelling, as local history and community-specific, has been studied in the works of Keith Basso[17] and Charles Briggs[18] – to mention just two names. As the research of these anthropologists shows, and as I will discuss further in this article, the specificity of narration is also geographical. Place names, historical events and personal memories related to places are recurrent topics in Sámi storytelling. As attachment to the land is relevant to the identity management of a culture in a ongoing process of revitalisation, the investigation of place-making strategies in contemporary narratives is also important.

Finally, I approach storytelling as a source of knowledge in outreach initiatives. Recent productions and their accessibility through new media imply that the audience targeted by Sámi productions is not exclusively the community but in fact much broader. Changing attitudes towards a language and a group is part of the revitalisation process[19] and one of

14 Lenore Grenoble and Lindsay Whaley, *Saving Languages: An Introduction to Language Revitalization* (Cambridge, 2006).

15 Sari Pietikäinen, 'Broadcasting Indigenous Voices: Sami Minority Media Production', *European Journal of Communication* 23 (2) (2008), pp. 173-191.

16 Haley de Korne, 'Indigenous Language Education Policy: Supporting Community-Controlled Immersion in Canada and the US', *Language Policy* 9 (2010), pp. 115-141.

17 Keith Basso, *Wisdom Sits in Places: Landscape and Language Among the Western Apache* (Albuquerque, 1996).

18 Charles Briggs, *Competence in Performance: the Creativity of Tradition in Mexican Verbal Art* (Philadelphia, 1988).

19 Grenoble and Whaley, *Saving Languages*, p. 13.

the goals of contemporary minority politics. Here I will illustrate to what extent storytelling can contribute to achieving these aims.

Storytelling and endangered languages

As Sari Pietikäinen emphasises in her research about Sámi revitalisation, language is 'the essential marker of the indigenous identity'.[20] It is also a vehicle for the transmission of knowledge, for example, that embedded in narratives. This significance of language was observed one hundred years ago by philologists interested in Sámi culture and traditions. These lappologists' predilection for legends and tales when collecting language samples in the late 1800s and early 1900s has given today's scholars a rich and extensive corpus of Sámi narratives. The term lappology was coined from the word used to refer to the Sámi at that time – 'Lapp' – which did not have the negative connotation it has today. Nevertheless, it does refer to the Sámi as a foreign object. The term and the field of research reflect how the Sámi lacked the capability to influence what was occurring at the time. The main concern of the lappologists was to document language and culture before they vanished. The principal aim was to collect as much as possible, as was done, for example, by the scholars Just K. Qvigstad and Eliel Lagercrantz[21] at the turn of the twentieth century. They published a wide collection of texts from most parts of Sápmi, in an attempt to preserve Sámi languages.

While the prediction that the languages would become extinct did not come true, today the Sámi languages are endangered. The UNESCO *Atlas of the World's Languages in Danger*[22] places ten Sámi languages on a scale of endangerment that has five levels, from vulnerable to extinct. Akkala Sámi, originally spoken in the Kola Peninsula is listed as 'extinct'. Pite, Ume and Ter Sámi are 'critically endangered', which according to UNESCO criteria means that the youngest speakers are grandparents or older, who only speak the language partially and infrequently. South, Lule, Skolt, Inari and Kildin Sámi are estimated to be 'severely endangered', that is, they are spoken by grandparents and older generations, with the parent generation

20 Pietikäinen, 'Broadcasting Indigenous Voices'.

21 Eliel Lagercrantz, *Lappische Volksdichtung*, vol. II (Helsinki, 1958); Just Knud Qvigstad, *Lappiske eventyr och sagn I-IV* (Oslo, 1927-1929).

22 UNESCO, *Atlas of the World's Languages in Danger*, http://www.unesco.org/new/en/culture/themes/endangered-languages/, accessed July 19, 2012.

perhaps understanding the language but not speaking it to their children or among themselves. The most spoken Sámi language, North Sámi, is listed by UNESCO as 'definitely endangered', the second lowest level of endangerment, characterised by the fact that children no longer learn the language as a mother tongue at home.

The narratives collected one hundred years ago by lappologists are today being reactualised for language revitalisation. Although their work was affected by the bias of the ideological context of their time, this collection of data is valuable to today's researchers as a testimony of a time of social change.[23] In addition, the corpus that they compiled shows how storytelling was used as a tool to preserve and promote languages. Moreover, recent productions make use of Sámi narratives with reference to older sources published by lappologists and early Sámi writers.[24]

Such examples can be found in co-productions by the Sámi Education Centre in Jokkmokk and the Swedish Educational Broadcasting Company. Sites for language acquisition[25] include narratives for practising listening comprehension. On the Gulahalan site, for instance, we find 'traditional Sámi stories', that is, readings from an early collection of North Sámi legends by Qvigstad and from a publication by the storyteller Johan Turi. The digital narrative 'Cugu' is yet another example in which the producer John Erling Utsi refers to the long storytelling tradition of his community.[26] Other instances of digital environments making use of Sámi storytelling can be found on the Sámi radio website.[27] Thus, most Sámi are familiar with traditional characters in storytelling such as Stállu, an evil and silly ogre who hunts young Sámi children, and the underground beings, the *háldit*, or the

---

23 Coppelie Cocq, *Revoicing Sámi Narratives. North Sámi Storytelling at the Turn of the 20th Century* (Umeå, 2008).

24 For instance Anta Pirak, *Jåhttee saamee viessoom* (Uppsala, 1937); Johan Turi, *Muittalus Samid Birra* (Stockholm, 1910).

25 Utbildningsradion, 'Gulahalan', http://www4.ur.se/gulahalan/, accessed July 10, 2012; Utbildningsradion, 'Cugu', http://www.ur.se/cugu/, accessed July 10, 2012; Utbildningsradion, 'Sámásta', http://www.ur.se/samasta/, accessed July 10, 2012.

26 Sameradion, 'Cugu'- ny barnradio (January 12, 2010), http://sverigesradio.se/sida/artikel.aspx?programid=2327&artikel=3365060, accessed July 10, 2012.

27 Sameradion, 'Noaidegiisá', http://sverigesradio.se/sida/default.aspx?programid=3124, accessed July 10, 2012; *Sameradion*, 'Giehto Tjärrováres', http://sverigesradio.se/sida/gruppsida.aspx?programid=3967&grupp=13550, accessed July 10, 2012.

čuđit, who are plunderers and the enemies of the Sámi. Stories about these characters can be found in most collections of Sámi folklore.

This illustration was made by Merja Aletta Ranttila and is a creation of imagination and partly based on the traditional stories told about the Stállu character.
Source: http://www.samimuseum.fi/maahisweb/sapmi/sa_poikajastaalo.html.

In the Sámi context, the number of occurrences of storytelling is increasing and there is an attempt to include different Sámi languages – though North Sámi is by far the most represented and visible. These initiatives represent contemporary narrative practices for pedagogical purposes, in line with the function of narration observed in previous research. In a study of the upbringing of Sámi children, Asta Balto[28] emphasised the role of storytelling, arguing that cultural transmission takes place through narration, where the atmosphere and excitement may be as important as the story itself.[29] Narratives tell us about people's relationship to nature and provide examples of good and bad behaviour. Balto's observations, based on fieldwork conducted in the mid-1980s, are still valid when studying contemporary storytelling in 2012. The continuity and the educational function of traditional legends and tales are still strongly apparent.

28 Asta Balto, *Samisk barneoppdragelse i endring* (Oslo, 1997); Asta Balto, 'Upbringing for Self-esteem, Zest for Life and Joy', in: *Woman in a Northern Landscape* (Nordfold, 1999).

29 Balto, *Samisk barneoppdragelse*, p. 92.

However, since the new legislation, a further dimension has been added – Sámi productions now follow a specific agenda, that is, minority politics. The educational purpose of legends and tales today is still central, although a shift has occurred from the transmission of tacit knowledge to the explicit goal of language acquisition. The adjustment to the audience, as well as the role of media in the politics of minority languages, have led to the predominance of a didactic goal in the contemporary forms of storytelling, with the content and the composition of the stories designed to promote language acquisition.

The development of digital productions has gained attention in the field of education, and the explicit goal and didactic efforts have made digitally based storytelling a source of knowledge for language learners and young children in classrooms. Such storytelling, as a tool for teaching and promoting languages, has a strong potential, not least in multimedia format that enables the combination of simultaneously diverse exercises to practise several skills, such as listening, communicating and reading. Thus, it is a means for the strengthening, promotion and development of minor and endangered languages. Moreover, as I discuss in the following section, storytelling also plays a significant role in identity management through another aspect – also embedded in language – that is, the place-making strategies of narration.

Storytelling and place-making

Previous research in anthropology has emphasised the significance of place and place-making. For example, Julie Cruikshank has investigated the cultural and regional aspects of storytelling and the naming of places,[30] while from a broader perspective, Tim Ingold's research demonstrates how our interaction with nature is reflected in livelihoods, housing patterns and practical skills.[31] His anthropological approach shows how people's relationships to nature are reflected in world-views, traditions and approaches to the human, the natural and the spiritual.

In the same vein, Basso discusses people's relationships to specific places

30 Julie Cruikshank, 'Getting the Words Right: Perspectives on Naming and Places in Athapaskan Oral History', *Arctic Anthropology* 27 (1) (1990), pp. 52-65.

31 Tim Ingold, *The Perception of Environment: Essays on Livelihood, Dwelling and Skill* (London, 2000); Tim Ingold, 'Conversations from the North', in: Paula Kaankanpää et al., eds., *Knowledge and Power in the Arctic* (Rovaniemi, 2007), pp. 11-15.

focusing on Apache narratives, place-names and patterns of speech and language. He claims that stories articulate a description of the relationship to the land and the past that underscores continuity, or, in Basso's words, 'place-making is a way to construct history itself'.[32] From this perspective, the narratives of indigenous and minority peoples comprise valuable knowledge about the land that is maintained through time and conveyed from generation to generation.

For indigenous people, the land is not only a place of longing and belonging,[33] it is also associated with history, culture and legal rights. This is articulated in Sámi identity discourse, where one's place of origin, genealogy and ancestors define one's position within the community. Place-making is created through the narration of the names, memories, historical events and experiences connected to a specific place or landscape.

Throughout their adaptation to various temporal contexts, narratives maintain their strong attachment to the specific places they describe. The settings in legends and historical accounts, the descriptions of landscapes, which are points of reference for navigation, all contribute to place-making.[34] The role of the landscape and the significance given to a specific place in a legend or a historical account might change in a story told in different temporal contexts – but the place or the landscape remain the central elements in the story.

In such a way, narratives recorded by lappologists and written by early Sámi authors are witness to the reciprocal significance of places and narration. For example, Turi provides an explanation for the name of the mountain Báhcajeagil:

> And on the eastern side of the southern tip of Stálojávri there is a mountain called Báhcajeagil. And it got its name because the best lichen [*jeagil*] used to grow there. And people would say 'The lichen has stayed [*báhcán*] on this mountain.' And so it got the name Báhcánjeagil [that is, Stayed lichen], and that is its name even today, Báhcajeagil.[35]

32 Basso, *Wisdom*, p. 7.

33 Ibidem.

34 See, for example Franz Boas, *Geographical Names of the Kwakiutl Indians* (New York, 1934).

35 Johan Turi, *An Account of the Sámi* (Chicago, 2011), p. 143.

Bookcover by Johan Turi.
Source: http://inemarit.wordpress.com/2010/04/24/muitalus-samiid-birra-den-f%C3%B8rste-boka-pa-samisk/.

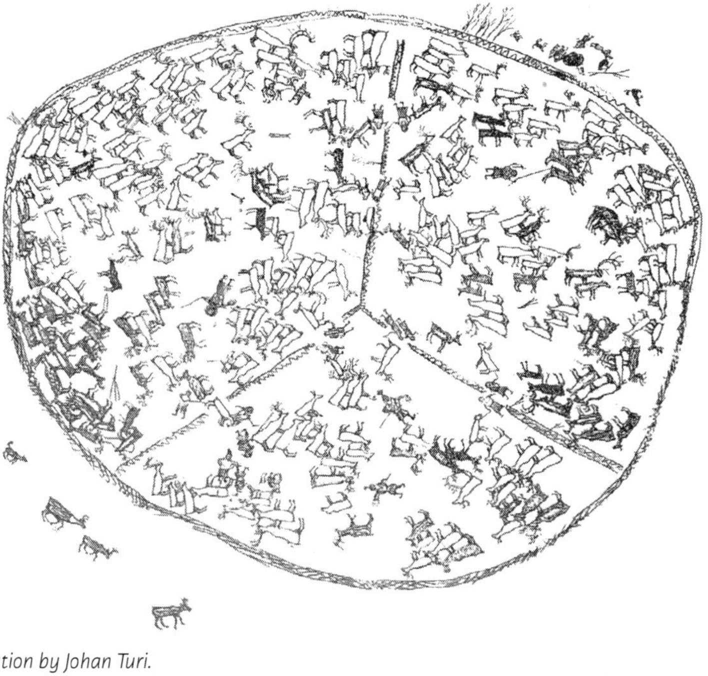

Illustration by Johan Turi.
Source: http://ookaboo.com/o/pictures/picture/21528045/Muitalus_s%C3%A1miid_birra_by_Johan_Turi.

American folklorist Thomas DuBois has emphasised the role of landscape in Sámi legends.[36] In many instances, the hero manages to dupe his enemies due to his knowledge of the topography. The persistent attachment to the land is a key element of the storytelling tradition and a source of information for members of the community.

In more recent adaptations of storytelling, the landscape also has a prominent role. In the digital narrative 'Cugu',[37] for example, the story takes us through the landscape over the course of different events and challenges. The focus is on nature, the mountains, the animals and beings from Sámi stories that inhabit the landscape.

Another example of contemporary storytelling is 'Giehto Tjärrovάres',[38] a series of stories in Lule Sámi. The point of departure of the narratives is a specific place, Luovvaluokta and its inhabitants. From this basis, the programme develops using audio files as well as photos and illustrations by Lennart Pirtsi, one of the storytellers. Thus, the programme is built upon a specific place.

Indigenous knowledge is also embedded in maps; for example, in relation to resources and watercourses. Legends, tales, memories and historical narratives tell us the meaning of the place names, being named after people, the way they were used or because of the things they resemble. Narration passes on knowledge about places, their origin and the history associated with them. Moreover, the stories tell us about the values of the community, for example, regarding subsistence and resources, and about a community's relationship to the land and the sea.[39]

Our dependence upon nature today is not as crucial as in times and places where technology and infrastructure were not available. Therefore, knowledge about navigation and resources is not essential to survival to the same extent. Nevertheless, the transmission of this knowledge still takes place through narratives and has a function in contemporary Sápmi. The shape of a lake provides the context for a story about Stállu, while

36 Thomas DuBois, 'Insider and Outsider: An Inari Saami Case', *Scandinavian Studies* 67 (1) (1995), pp. 63-76.

37 UR, 'Cugu'.

38 UR, 'Giehto Tjärrováres'.

39 See Ann Fienup-Riordan, ed., *Qaluyaarmiuni Nunamtenek Qanemciput/Our Nelson Island Stories: Meanings of Place of the Bering Sea Coast*, translated by Alice Rearden (Seattle, 2011).

a red-coloured cliff provides the occasion for a tale about the *čuđit* and how the Sámi defeated them.[40] Narratives describing the landscape and the origin of place names create a reference to a common history and to ancestors. In contemporary Sámi discourses and in narratives, the land is 'a central unifying and meaning making element'.[41]

As illustrated above, contemporary Sámi storytelling, through its role in language practice and acquisition, plays a significant role in the articulation of Sámi identities. In a similar manner, the place-making strategies of Sámi narratives contribute to the strengthening of identity through the articulation of a common history and geographical roots. If storytelling constitutes a vehicle for knowledge essential to the community members, it might also convey knowledge about the Sámi to a broader audience.

Storytelling as a source of knowledge

Traditional narratives from older sources are emerging in contemporary contexts, in new media and with a new purpose – that of language acquisition. However, the continuity of geographical settings in legends and historical accounts indicate that place-making strategies are still prevalent and of significance for the Sámi community. The use of different media for the diffusion and consumption of recent narratives implies that the possibilities and opportunities to reach an audience outside the community itself have increased. In fact, this is both an inevitable side effect and an advantage of mass media and the internet. Therefore, the meanings, functions and purposes of Sámi storytelling for the non-Sámi audience must be taken into consideration in an investigation of storytelling in a revitalisation context.

The relationship and overlap between inreach and outreach productions and their implications for indigenous people have been discussed by Kyra Landzelius.[42] Community inreach initiatives, such as

40 Turi, *Muittalus Samid Birra*, p. 151; Krister Stoor, 'Bakhållet vid Lappskottbacken. En berättelse om "de främmande" i en samisk miljö', in: Jurij Kusmenko, ed., *The Sámi and the Scandinavians. Aspects of 2000 Years of Contact* (Hamburg, 2004), pp. 73-87.

41 DuBois, 'Insider and Outsider', p. 75 (observation based on Inari Sámi narratives).

42 Kyra Landzelius, ed., *Native on the Net: Indigenous and Diasporic Peoples in the Virtual Age* (London, 2006).

the efforts being made to teach language online and increase the extent to which information is accessible, pertain 'to localized interests, with the dissemination of ingroup information (...) as well as the import of expert knowledge to the local level'.[43] The examples of narratives mentioned above, such as 'Cugu' and those found on the Gulahalan site and the 'Giehto Tjärrovàres' programme, represent such efforts.

Outreach initiatives, on the other hand, are characterised by a 'tourist' perspective, addressing a non-indigenous audience. However, as Landzelius pertinently points out, 'mixed genres of usage' imply 'that sometimes the best inreach might be via outreach'.[44] Inreach and outreach efforts are in most cases intertwined in such a way that it is difficult to establish a clear distinction, for example, the audience for online and mass media products is very likely to be composed of users with various backgrounds, knowledge, expectations and interests.

The Sámi storytelling tradition is often presented as a central aspect of Sámi culture and it is used in many contemporary representations of the Sámi.[45] From this perspective and bearing in mind the increased opportunities for indigenous initiatives in the contemporary legislative context, we ought to consider how storytelling today may constitute a source of knowledge about Sámi culture and language. Contemporary adaptations and productions lead to increased visibility of the Sami and greater accessibility to information and knowledge about them for a broader audience. Thus, narratives are not only a means of language acquisition and the articulation of identity, but also a means of articulation of knowledge about history, traditions and culture.

Firstly, storytelling provides access to historical knowledge that has not been included in history books. In Scandinavia, as in many other parts of the world, minority groups have long been excluded, neglected or forgotten in accounts of national history. While the lack of documentation about the Sámi minority and the lack of an emic perspective on historical events and social change cannot be adequately rectified, traces of these events and perspectives can be found in narratives. Storytelling emerges from social life and is constructed, reproduced and adapted by members of the

43 Landzelius, *Native on the Net*, p. 9.

44 Ibidem, p. 10.

45 Coppelie Cocq, 'Anthropological Places, Digital Spaces and Imaginary Spaces', *Folklore* 124 (forthcoming, 2013).

community. Therefore, the analysis of narratives enables us to gain insight into how significant aspects of social life are experienced by the community. The use of storytelling as a way of making the minority's voice heard was one of the aims of the first Sámi writer, Turi.[46] Today, his narratives, as well as recorded accounts by elders, are a source of knowledge that gives us a version of history in the voices of those previously neglected. The texts we have access to today are a testament to Sámi historical events as they were experienced by the community, and that have been preserved from oral history in written versions.

Johan Turi (1854-1936), the first Sámi writer. Photograph by Borg Mesch (1869-1956). Source: http://www.theapricity.com/forum/showthread.php?p=473363.

Secondly, storytelling is a means of empowerment. In the context of revitalisation this is a significant aspect of minority discourses which should be taken into consideration. Along with Jan Servaes, we can observe how culture is the arena of the struggle for empowerment.[47] The opportunities

46 Turi, *Muittalus.*

47 Jan Servaes, *Communication for Development: One World, Multiple Cultures* (Cresskill, 1999).

for Sámi agents to participate in the shaping of representations have increased thanks to ideological, political and technical developments which have made it possible for new actors to make their voices heard. The Sámi can now contribute to a greater extent to the production of knowledge about their own culture and history. Initiatives from Sámi officials have also resulted in better visibility of the Sámi cultures and traditions.

The potential of storytelling as a source of knowledge has increased due to new modes of mediation and transmission. Nevertheless, we should remember the limits of visibility and the complexity of representing a heterogeneous group such as the Sámi. Media, that is, new media, mass media and the internet, is a tool in the elaboration of a shared identity. However, a point of friction in Sámi media is that 'not all Sami people speak indigenous languages leaving a considerable proportion of the people outside the mediated community'.[48] Moreover, a North Sámi-oriented perspective currently prevails in contemporary Sámi productions. On a broader – global level – it is also apparent that while well-documented languages with the greatest number of speakers (among minority communities) remain stronger, there is still a lot to be done for critically and severely endangered languages.

Concluding remarks

At the turn of the twentieth century, legends and tales gave expression to and articulated social change. One hundred years later, narratives appear central to processes of cultural and linguistic revitalisation. Storytelling as an oral tradition, as written literature or digitally mediated, has been, is and will most likely remain a significant tool in the struggle of minorities to articulate their identities and find empowerment.

Topics in storytelling emerge in different temporal contexts; thus, narratives similar in content can express different discourses, being modified and adapted to contemporary circumstances. Traces of historical events emerge in narratives told in different periods of time, in stories which have been narrated through the generations. The persistence of these narratives demonstrates their significance despite changes in content. Thus, the lappologists were told particular versions of these stories, in which, for example, legends about enemies might have different

48 Pietikäinen, 'Broadcasting Indigenous Voices', p. 188.

warning functions and may represent different dangers at different periods of time; nevertheless, they emerge as central to the contemporary Sámi community in articulating their distinctiveness and a sense of belonging. Today, the context may differ, and there might be other threats and enemies, but the community may retain the 'same attitudes and same goal in telling today's legends, anecdotes and jokes'.[49]

By approaching Sámi narratives in a historical and contemporary perspective, this article shows how the practices of storytelling have evolved in accordance with changes in premises and the nature of audiences. Despite these variations, storytelling is central, articulating topics of significance to the community. In other words, storytelling is still a mode of communication and of production of knowledge, a mode of negotiation and of elaboration of identity.

This study illustrates how storytelling can be a strong and effective means of language reinforcement and renewal. Due to its power of adaptation, storytelling has become one important tool in revitalisation efforts. The didactic qualities of narrative practices and the inherent capability of new media to adapt and create have made storytelling a rich tool for language teaching and acquisition.

Moreover, a historical and contemporary perspective on Sámi storytelling highlights the continuity of place-making strategies. The knowledge embedded in place names and conveyed through narratives, the stories connected to the landscape and the narrative mapping of the use of a specific space, are part of the collective identity. Narratives about the land and the landscape are significant to identity management for members of the indigenous community. Furthermore, storytelling constitutes an important and often unexploited source of knowledge. As a source, storytelling is a spring which produces knowledge that is not accessible elsewhere. As a resource, it is also a place to go back to and to renegotiate in order to create continuity. Thus, storytelling represents a place for negotiation and empowerment.

49 Lassi Saressalo, 'The Threat from Without', in: Tore Ahlbäck, ed., *Saami Religion* (Åbo, 1987), p. 255.

Translation History: Between Micro- and Macro-narratives

« Cees Koster »

When writing a history of translation you have to find a frame of reference and make choices. You have to find your way into the entire labyrinth of the dynamics of transnational reception and translation, of the wide range of relevant agents and institutions, of events, incidents, moments, actions, behaviour and texts (both the translations themselves and their satellite texts: paratexts, poetical texts).[1]

One obvious frame of reference that limits and may guide one's choices is that of the nation. However, if you wish to write the history of literary translation of a single receiving culture, the frame immediately widens again: you have to deal with at least three historiographic disciplines: translation history, reception history and literary history.

In this paper I will look into some of the problems of writing such a history, from a practical as well as a theoretical point of view. The practical questions to be discussed are: What is a workable format for such an undertaking? What kind of ordering principles should be used? What kind of priorities should be set? The theoretical questions concern the justification of a historiographical framework that may account for a proper contextualisation of the phenomenon of translation.

From a practical point of view, my own interest in the subject lies in my involvement in the realisation of a project aiming at publishing a comprehensive history of literary translation into Dutch from the Middle

1 Cf. Cees Koster and Ton Naaijkens, 'Translators in Translation History – The Dutch Case'. Paper presented to *The Fifth Biennial Conference of the American Translation & Interpreting Studies Association 'The Sociological Turn in Translation and Interpreting Studies'*. April 24, 2010.

Ages to the present in a single volume of about 600 pages, to be published in 2014.[2]

The main justification for the project is the circumstance that no such book exists and that it is long overdue. Comprehensive national translation histories seem to be a rarity in any case. Pym, in his seminal book on translation history,[3] gives an overview of the histories he is aware of and most of them seem to be geographically of a broader scope and/or temporally restricted to specific periods. However, there are some models, most notably one on the history of translation in Spain[4] and two about literary translation into English.[5]

In a sense one might say that as far as literature is concerned, the most natural context of a project such as this is the framework of national literary history.[6] From the point of view of Translation Studies this may seem obvious, at least if one adheres to the idea that the field of translation is embedded within the larger literary, cultural, economic and political fields of the receiving culture. From the point of view of literary history this is not all that obvious.

2 The project in question involves the production of a broad, comprehensive and varied history of translation in the Low Countries from the Middle Ages to the present. Joint editors of the project are Theo Hermans (University College London), Ton Naaijkens and myself (Utrecht University). The views expressed in this article are my own.

3 Anthony Pym, *Method in Translation History* (Manchester, 1998), pp. 9-10, 13.

4 Francisco Lafarga and Luis Pegenaute, eds., *Historia de la traducción en España* (Salamanca, 2004).

5 Peter France, ed., *The Oxford Guide to Literature in English Translation* (New York, 2000); Olive Classe, *Encyclopedia of Literary Translation into English* (London, 2000); cf. also Dirk Delabastita, 'From Aesop to Zweig and From Martial to Martial Arts Fiction: Charting the History of Literary Translation into English', *Target* 1 (2002), pp. 149-171.

6 Perhaps it is appropriate to insert a caveat at this point. I do realise that the concepts of 'nation' and 'literature' are problematic because their conceptualisations are not a-historical or a-cultural. In a historical project that deals with such a long period, this problematic status becomes even more acute. The geographical area that is dealt with in this project comprises what are now known as the Netherlands and Flanders. The translational history is not confined to literature per se, at least not in any restricted conceptualisation. The considerations in this article, however, will focus on the translation and reception of literature.

An old complaint, mainly from within the disciplines of Comparative Literature and Translation Studies, is that most historiographic approaches to literature have shown themselves to be blind to the role and position of translation (and, by extension, foreign literature) within the domain of a national literature. This situation seems to be changing, however, with the role of translation as a constitutive factor in societies and cultures being increasingly acknowledged. One example from the domain of cultural history is Peter Burke, who, in his *Lost and Found in Translation: A Cultural History of Translators and Translating in Early Modern Europe*, states 'that history deserves a large place in Translation Studies and that studies of translation deserve a large place in history. Translation is actually central to cultural history'.[7]

In a recent issue of the Dutch journal of Literary Studies *Nederlandse Letterkunde*, the guest editors of a special edition on the reception and translation of foreign literature in the Netherlands show that as far as the historiography of Dutch literature is concerned, the old situation still prevails. According to them, however, 'the presence of foreign literature to a large extent has affected the national literary field' and 'what is characteristic and remarkable about Dutch literature might be better reflected in research efforts directed at how this literature is embedded in an international framework and to what interactions occurred with foreign literatures'.[8]

The most recent major effort in Dutch literary history still fails to include translation and transnational literary exchange as a separate topic in its eight volumes.[9] In some of the volumes it is almost impossible to ignore translation (as an umbrella term for all the guises under which the phenomenon occurs) because in the period in question (most notably of course the Middle Ages and the Early Modern Period) the difference between original literature and different forms of productive reception

7 Peter Burke, *Lost (and Found) in Translation: A Cultural History of Translators and Translating in Early Modern Europe* (Wassenaar, 2005); cf. also Peter Burke and Ronnie Po-Chia Hsia, eds., *Cultural Translation in Early Modern Europe* (Cambridge, 2007).

8 Els Andringa, Sophie Levie and Mathijs Sanders, 'Het buitenland bekeken. Vijf internationale auteurs door Nederlandse ogen (1900-2000)', *Nederlandse Letterkunde* 3 (2006), p. 199.

9 *Geschiedenis van de Nederlandse literatuur* was initiated by the Nederlandse Taalunie, and is a combined effort of Dutch and Flemish authors.

were not as clear cut as they may seem today. However, in the volumes on the nineteenth and twentieth centuries, even though the relationships between Dutch and foreign literatures is acknowledged, they are not discussed. In a sense, then, our translational history may be seen as a companion volume to this literary history.

Another series to which the history may be considered a companion volume is 'Dutch Discourses on Translation' a six-volume series of anthologies with annotated texts on translation poetics or aesthetics from the Middle Ages to the twentieth century. Obviously, anthologised texts cannot do without contextualisation, but an anthology has limited historiographic possibilities. Together, the introductions to the volumes may be considered as a concise history of the Dutch discourse on translation, but there remains much more to say.

As far as periodisation is concerned, our comprehensive history more or less follows the anthology series. Periodisation obviously is a basic ordering principle for such a project, both from a methodological and practical point of view. According to Foz, 'we know [periodisation] to be indispensible, though at times it can also be problematic because it is so systematic'.[10] The problem Foz refers to is that any periodisation implies some kind of discontinuity between periods that more often than not cannot be justified. This problem may be more acute when periodisation is based on a temporal division rather than on thematic grounds. In this project we still opted for a more traditional periodisation: separate chapters will be devoted to the Middle Ages (to 1550), the Early Modern Period (1550-1800), the Nineteenth Century, the First Half of the Twentieth Century, and the Second Half of the Twentieth Century. The big advantage here is that a more thematically oriented division into periods (Classicism, Enlightenment, Romanticism, Modernism for instance) already presupposes (and therefore might privilege) specific ways of thinking about translation. The more traditional division allows ample room for presenting and confronting mainstream and peripheral voices and discourses.

Within the chapters devoted to specific periods, however, the selection and ordering of the wealth of potential material is more complicated. One of the first problems pertains to the claim of comprehensiveness. To a certain extent it might be said that there is an inherent tension between the claim to comprehensiveness and the fundamental impossibility of

10 Clara Foz, 'Translation, History and the Translation Scholar', in: Georges Bastin and Paul Bandia, eds., *Charting the Future of Translation History* (Ottawa, 2006), p. 136.

substantiating it. Then why put forward the claim? Perhaps this question can best be answered by discussing the relationship between historical micro- and macro-narratives.

That writing history is basically narrative in nature may today be seen as a truism; the real question is, What kind of narrative? Surely not a grand narrative, as a another truism goes – a narrative that aspires to comprehensive explanatory hypotheses. The alternative is to focus on micro-narratives, if you will, each of which looks at a certain phenomenon from a certain perspective (or research question) that provides its own pertinence or sense of relevance. The sort of criticism that this type of focus is prone to, as has been shown to be the case for a Dutch history *Nederlandse literatuur, een geschiedenis* edited by Schenkeveld-van der Dussen and a recent American literary history, *A New Literary History of America* edited by Marcus & Sollors, is that of conceptual discontinuity.

Our historiographical enterprise will aim at the best of both worlds: we will try to be comprehensive, with all the methodological caveats in place, not by writing a single macro-history, but by oscillating between macro-narrative contextualisation and case-study-like micro-narratives, between single comprehensive chapters for each period and a whole range of micro-narratives.

The claim of the comprehensive chapters is that they will give an overview of developments and changes in the field of translation in the given period, and they will deal with issues of broader scope and scale concerning the material and cultural context of translation, both quantitatively and qualitatively. They will cover (i) the material and institutional conditions of translation, including markets, production centres and importation and distribution channels, the volume of translations produced, the social composition of the readership and translation aids such as glossaries, dictionaries and training facilities; (ii) the identity and social status of translators, including translators' contacts, networks and self-descriptions; (iii) prevailing ideas and discourses about translation, including criticism and polemics; (iv) the changing practices of translation, including main source languages and genres and major translators and translations; and (v) the wider social and intellectual impact of translation.

For the shorter pieces a whole range of different foci is available that can be taken as a staring point for a single narrative, the most obvious being a single translator in his or her role of cultural mediator, a specific single source text, source author or source culture, publishers of translated literature, and the presence and role of translation in certain genres and domains (poetry, the historical novel, ancient literature, crime novel, literature for children and young adults, science, etc.).

There are obvious practical advantages to this classification of foci, but it also has a theoretical bearing. Each of the foci allows for an approach in which both poetical and institutional factors are given due attention. For translation to be dealt with comprehensively as a cultural phenomenon it is necessary to use a framework that is able to encompass all relevant aspects of translation, both on the institutional and the aesthetic levels, with respect to both context and text.

Dante Alighieri (1265-1321).
Source: http://illavorodelloscrittore.wordpress.com/2012/03/18/dante-alighieri-commedia-poema-ebook/.

In what remains I would like to exemplify these theoretical considerations by presenting the outline of a hypothetical case (translations of Dante's *Divine Comedy* in the latter half of the nineteenth century) and illustrate the methodological and practical choices that have to be made with respect to this material in terms of its institutional and poetical implications, and with respect to the question of what aspects may best be discussed in the macro-narrative and which in a micro-narrative. The choice of this material is relatively arbitrary and mainly informed by methodological considerations, but it still concerns a relatively restricted area (in terms of period and source language), which means that not every aspect may be extrapolated into more general principles.

To a certain extent, every historical narrative is first and foremost informed by the material and documentation available. Pym[11] makes a distinction between catalogue and corpus; catalogue being the bibliographical list in its entirety and corpus being the translations chosen for a specific case study. In the catalogue of the translation history of Dante's *Divina Commedia* in Dutch, the corpus of a case study on the latter half of the nineteenth century consists of five translations: four complete and one of the first book only: 'Hell'.

Year of publication	Translated text	Translator	Publisher
1863-1864	Divine Comedy	A.S. Kok	Haarlem: Kruseman
1867-1873	Divine Comedy	J.C. Hacke van Mijnden	Haarlem: Kruseman
1874	Divine Comedy	U.W. Thoden van Velzen	Leeuwarden: Jongbloed
1877	Hell	J.J.L. ten Kate	Leiden: Sijthoff
1876-1884	Divine Comedy	Joan Bohl	Haarlem: De Graaff

Around this corpus a wealth of supplementary documentation may be collected on the translators and publishers, on the reception of the translations and on the non-translatory reception of Dante and the *Divine Comedy* in order to contextualise the bare data in the table.

Out of this wealth I will select two aspects for discussion that would typically belong to a macro-narrative, one pertaining to institutional issues, one to aesthetics.

Two of the more interesting aspects of the macro-narrative on the nineteenth century as a whole concern the questions of why there was such frantic activity in the field of Dante translation in this period and why the first translation was published only some five and a half centuries after the original.

These questions are hard to answer directly, as they involve discerning intentions and motivations that are difficult to reconstruct; however, there are some general tendencies in the fields of literature and translation, and in Dutch society as a whole, that may provide some explanation of why at that point in time the Dutch field became susceptible to the translations of Dante's classic poem.

From the point of view of literary evolution, the later reception of Dante is related to the emergence of Romanticism. The first Dutch translation may have been late in coming, although its path was paved by the translation of separate passages in several literary magazines, but it was only relatively late in comparison to Dante translations into other European languages.

11 Pym, *Method*, p. 42.

Data provided by Van Heck show that the first German translation was published in 1767-1769, the first English in 1802, and the first French in 1811-1813.[12] According to Van den Berg,[13] Dante, just as Shakespeare, was one of the postclassical authors who came to be associated with the term 'Romanticism'. In that sense the publication date of the first Dutch translation accords with the general trend. In the historiography of Dutch literature it is generally agreed upon that the emergence of Romanticism was postponed: there may have been an 'early' diluted form of Romanticism in the 1830s but it did not last very long; it was not until the 1880s that a 'real' romantic movement is supposed to have emerged.[14] This is not to say that any of the Dante translations played a role in this emergence, as most of the translators can be considered pre-romantics, but the general climate must have been one of a growing susceptibility, which may in part explain the boom. Another part of the explanation may be found in the state of Dutch society at the time.

During the first half of the nineteenth century, conservatism and complacency seemed to be the defining characteristics of Dutch society, but in the second half of the nineteenth century the Netherlands saw several profound economic, social and cultural changes that turned it into a modern country: industrialisation became more intense, economic activity grew and infrastructure improved.[15] Important political European reforms were also introduced into the Dutch system. There were also several educational reforms that led to increased participation in education by the middle class. Thus, a large middle class was developing, whose members were on average better educated and had more money to spend than previously.

12 Paul van Heck, 'Ciò che poeta la lingua nostra. One Hundred and More Years of Dante Translations into Dutch', in: Ronald de Rooy, ed., *Divine Comedies for the New Millenium. Recent Dante Translations in America and the Netherlands* (Amsterdam, 2003), p. 75.

13 Willem van den Berg, 'Romantiek in de Nederlandse letterkunde', in: Gerrit Jan van Bork and Nico Laan, *Twee eeuwen literatuurgeschiedenis. Poëticale opvattingen in de Nederlandse literatuur* (Groningen, 1986), p. 46.

14 Willem van den Berg, 'Nederlandse romantiek, een verschijnsel in de marge?', *De Gids* 2 (1990), pp. 126-135; cf. Cees Koster, *De Hollandsche Vertaalmolen. Nederlandse beschouwingen over vertalen, 1820-1885*. Reeks Vertaalhistorie, deel 5a (Den Haag, 2002).

15 For this overview cf. Cees Koster, 'Inleiding', in: Cees Koster, ed., *Tussen roem en vergetelheid. Terug naar de negentiende eeuw*, Filter 14 (3) (2007), pp. 3-4.

From the 1860s onwards, developments set in that would have consequences for the cultural and literary fields. Improved production methods in the publishing industry resulted in cheaper paper and printing techniques, which allowed publishers to sell their books and magazines at a cheaper rate and in higher numbers. Most publishers began to make use of series to market their products, most notable among them, series of foreign literature.[16]

As to the reading audience, several profound changes occurred as well. As mentioned, due to education reforms, participation in secondary education grew. In 1863 a new education law provided for a new form of secondary education – alongside the traditional Latin schools that led to academic study – to be established mainly for vocational purposes. In this new type of school, foreign languages and their literatures constituted a considerable part of the curriculum. Growing familiarity with foreign literature and writers led to an increase in the need for publications.

More importantly, however, the need for proper vocational training for the teachers of foreign languages led to a greater sense of professionalism and to the establishment of academic curricula in foreign languages. Teachers active in foreign language education, both in secondary as well as tertiary education, proved to be a great stimulus to Dutch cultural and literary life. Some of them were also active as translators and/or critics. One of the notable examples is A.S. Kok, responsible for the first translation of the *Divina Commedia* into Dutch, who taught English and Dutch in the new type of secondary school and was also self-educated in Italian.[17]

The story of the Dante translations, then, fits perfectly into the macro-narrative of literary and social changes in the latter half of the nineteenth century. As to the level of the micro-narrative, the contextualisation of the translators, either individually or as a group, is an obvious focus. From a broader point of view, Kok and Ten Kate are the more interesting candidates for a separate micro-narrative as they are the most prolific translators among the five. Kok not only was the first to translate the

16 Cf. Lisa Kuitert, *Het ene boek in vele delen. De uitgave van literaire series in Nederland 1850–1900* (Amsterdam, 1993).

17 Cf. Cees Koster, 'Fame and Fortune in the Field of Shakespeare Translation: the Case of A.S. Kok', in: Tom Toremans and Walter Verschueren, eds., *Crossing Cultures. Nineteenth-Century Anglophone Literature in the Low Countries* (Leuven, 2009), pp. 21-34.

Divina Commedia, but also the first to translate the complete dramatic works of Shakespeare into Dutch, albeit in prose. Nevertheless, he still remained a minor translator, mainly because he was eclipsed by others, his translations considered by his contemporaries to be aesthetically faulty.

Abraham Seyne Kok (1831-1915).
Source: http://www.geheugenvannederland.nl/?/nl/items/CBG01:11457.

The most interesting micro-narrative, however, would be about the polemical discussion between J.J.L. ten Kate and Joan Bohl on the aesthetics of metrical choices. Ten Kate's translation of *Inferno* was published just a year after Bohl´s first instalment of a complete translation appeared in 1876. Apparently Bohl was not amused, for he launched a virulent attack on Ten Kate's translation, or more specifically on his claim that the translation should be 'after the metre of the original'. Bohl's translation followed the Italian verse form, hendesyllabic lines with only feminine endings, while Ten Kate alternated between decasyllabic lines with masculine endings and hendesyllabic lines with feminine endings.

At that time, Ten Kate was one of the more famous Dutch poets, one of the leading so-called vicar-poets, and a prolific translator of Milton, Shakespeare and Goethe among others. He had the reputation of 'versificator', of clever poetaster, who would try his hand at anything, and he travelled the country to read his work to unusually large audiences. At first he was reluctant to produce a translation of Dante, but his publisher persuaded him with a handsome fee of several thousand guilders.

Anonymous portrait of Jan Jakob Lodewijk ten Kate (1819-1889).
Source: http://www.kb.nl/webexposities/nederlandse-literatuur/de-schepping.

Bohl was a lawyer by profession and by conviction a devout Catholic, as well as editor and founder of a Dutch journal on Dante, *De Wachter* [The Watchman/Gatekeeper]. In the field of translation and literature he was a relative outsider, although the combination of any civil job with literary activities was no exception at the time.

One can only speculate about the motives behind his attack, after all, Kok's translation made use of blank verse and Thoden van Velzen used rhymes only occasionally. Their polemic concentrates on the technical niceties of what a *terza rima* entails and on the question of whether the differences between Italian and Dutch versification force the translator to alternate between masculine and feminine rhyme, or whether it is a free choice of the translator. It is difficult to understand why both translators address each other so aggressively, unless one considers their dispute a discourse of legitimation, a battle for the title of representative of the 'true' Dante. If one takes this speculative explanation one step further, one might even look upon this polemic against the background of the struggle for Catholic emancipation in Dutch society in the latter half of the nineteenth century. The polemic would then be between a famous representative of the Protestant majority and a representative of the Catholic minority who is trying to claim the pre-Reformation author for his own ideological purposes.

This may be a form of speculative macro-historical contextualisation, but it shows how macro- and micro-narratives may contextualise each other and how micro- and macro-perspectives, so to speak, cannot do without each other. Any micro-narrative necessarily points to, or relates to, its broader context and any macro-narrative feeds on the material of micro-narratives. This may be taken as a further justification for using both perspectives.

Translations and Translators in Swedish Literary History

« Lars Kleberg »

It is a commonly cited notion that since the printing press came to Sweden – and actually even earlier – about half of all of the books published in Swedish have been translations.[1] With the strong exception of Sweden's period as a great power (*c.* 1600-1720), this fifty-fifty ratio between original and translated works has remained rather unchanged over the centuries.[2] Considering the fact that Sweden is and has been a translating country, an awareness of the vital role of translations in the evolution of Sweden's literature and culture in general is very limited. However, this has perhaps not always been the case. In this article, I will take a look at texts on the history of Swedish literature from different periods, focusing on a key period in the history of Swedish translation, the late eighteenth and early nineteenth centuries, and providing some comparisons and reflections. Recent examples of translation history from England and Finland will also be discussed. Finally, I will present some new contributions that are intended to provide the basis for a future history of Swedish translations.

The profound changes in the conditions governing cultural values and their forms of circulation, generally called globalisation, have as we know given the old concept of world literature or *Weltliteratur* a new topicality, with translations, the art of translation and its practitioners moving centre stage, into the light of critical and scholarly reflection. In Franco Moretti's

1 Lars Kleberg, 'Att göra översättningar synliga. Om översättningshistoria och databasen Svenskt översättarlexikon', in: Erland Jansson, ed., *En bok om böcker och bibliotek tillägnad Louise Brunes* (Huddinge, 2009), p. 173.

2 Cf. Lars Wollin's discussion of the question in 'Imperialism och xenofobi – eller ett öppet system. Kring ett brytningsskede i den svenska översättningens språkhistoria', at the 2010 IASS conference in Lund, 'Översättning – Adaption, Interpretation, Transformation'. The paper is available on Lars Wollin's homepage: http://www.larswollin.se, accessed August 1, 2012.

and Pascale Casanova's studies of the changes in the world literary system, for example, one is constantly reminded of and provoked to reflect on the dynamic role of translations.[3] Recent academic events such as the 2010 conference of the IASS in Lund devoted to different aspects of translation – including adaption, interpretation and transformation – are notable.[4] We are seeing a growing interest in world literature and questions concerning how the national – Swedish, Danish, Norwegian and Finland-Swedish – interacts with and is actually created by the encounter with the foreign.

A short digression on the position of world literature in literary history and literary scholarship in Sweden – in the academic discipline known as *litteraturvetenskap* – might be necessary in order to contextualise the following. Some ten years ago, a Nordic evaluation commissioned by the Swedish Council for Research in the Humanities and Social Sciences concluded that Swedish *litteraturvetenskap* was excellent in several aspects but hampered by its provincial or parochial limitations. The evaluators even called Swedish literature departments 'departments for the study of Swedish literature after 1930'.[5]

In Swedish research, the development of Sweden's literature has usually been seen as self-generating and endogenous. The focus on the modern was so striking that it provoked the evaluators to talk about a Swedish 'chronological myopia' or short-sightedness. If we make a simple diagram with a vertical time axis of 1600-2000 and a horizontal axis from provincial to global, one would find Swedish literary scholarship firmly positioned in the upper left corner.

3 Franco Moretti, *Graphs, Maps, Trees: Abstract Models for Literary History* (London, 2005); Pascale Casanova, *La république mondiale des lettres* (Paris, 1999).

4 Claes-Göran Holmberg and Per Erik Ljung, eds., *Översättning - adaption, interpretation, transformation: IASS 2010 proceedings: föredrag vid den 28:e studiekonferensen i International Association of Scandinavian Studies (IASS) i Lund 3-7 augusti 2010*, http://nile.lub.lu.se/ojs/index.php/IASS2010, accessed June 1, 2012. Selected papers, including a longer Swedish version of the present text, are published in: Per Erik Ljung, ed., *Transformationer: valda texter från International Association of Scandinavian Studies (IASS) 28:e konferens i Lund 2010* (Lund, 2011).

5 Bo Öhngren, *Litteraturforskningen i Sverige 1989-1996. En evaluering* (Stockholm, 2000), p. 51.

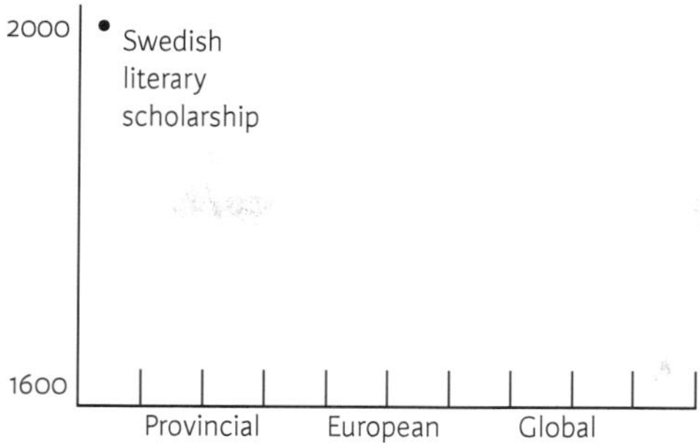

The Nordic evaluation was not received with unreserved enthusiasm in all Swedish literature departments, to say the least. In the past ten years, however, an obvious shift has taken place, especially on the geographical axis.

When we come to the field of translations, we see that the simple diagram sketched above does not suffice. A translated text, in principle, has two authors or two addressers: the author of the original source text and the translator. Whose words do we read in the translation, those of Shakespeare or of his Swedish translator Carl August Hagberg? Those of Homer or of his Swedish translator? In a way, both. In the terms of the Russian literary historian and philosopher Mikhail Bakhtin, a translation is decidedly a double-voiced text, where all the words of the source text can be considered as 'words of the other' included in one single utterance – that of the translator. From this perspective, rather than seeing the translation as simply a transparent 'package' or cover, we should see the utterance of the source text as intertwined with the target text.[6] Consequently, if we want to put translations into the above diagram as objects of study, we obviously have to follow the chronology of the translations, not of the originals. Studies of the Swedish Dante, Dostoevsky or Hölderlin would be placed on the chronological axis not according to when the source texts were written but when they were translated and read in the target culture.

In actual fact, contemporary Swedish literary historians would have almost nothing to offer with respect to translations and would be unable to locate them in a diagram such as the one above. Translations simply seem to fall outside their field of observation. Let us take one example. In the

6 Susanna Witt, 'Between the Lines: Totalitarianism and Translation in the USSR', in: Brian James Bear, ed., *Contexts, Subtexts, and Pretexts: Literary Translation in Eastern Europe and Russia* (Amsterdam/Philadelphia, 2011), pp. 152-153.

1840s, the Swedish professor of Modern Languages and Aesthetics at Lund University, Carl August Hagberg, published the first complete translation of Shakespeare's plays in Swedish. Hagberg's translations of the plays were performed and reprinted for almost 150 years, while quotations from his Shakespeare are used in contemporary everyday Swedish. However, to date there is not one academic article, not to mention a doctoral dissertation, about the work of someone who can rightly be called the most quoted author in Swedish literature. We think that we are quoting Shakespeare and tend to forget that at the same time we are actually quoting Hagberg. When I, some ten years ago, was looking for an article about Hagberg for the anthology *Med andra ord. Texter om litterär* översättning (In Other Words. Texts about Literary Translation) and turned to my academic colleagues at Stockholm University to ask where I should go, the Literature Department, the English Department and the Department of Scandinavian languages all pointed at each other.[7] Although this would not be the case today, the fact remains that we are still waiting for a dissertation about Hagberg's translations. A new, solid biography of Hagberg has appeared, but it does not deal specifically with his translations and their influence over the past 150 years.[8]

Carl August Hagberg (1810-1864).
Source: http://www.oversattarlexikon.se/artiklar/Carl_August_Hagberg.

7 Lars Kleberg, ed., *Med andra ord. Texter om litterär översättning* (repr. Stockholm, 2010).

8 Karin Monié, *Ord som himlen når. Carl August Hagberg – En levnadsteckning* (Stockholm, 2008).

In his book *The Translator's Invisibility. A History of Translation*, Lawrence Venuti has strongly criticised the dominant ideology of translation in the Anglo-American world. According to Venuti, the work of translators is made invisible in English and American culture by two interacting factors. The first is a resistance to incoming translations, apparent in the fact that so few translations are published in the United Kingdom and the United States in comparison with the great number of works that are exported, that is, translated from English. According to Venuti's figures, translation makes up only slightly more than 2 percent of the total book production in the United States, whereas the corresponding figures for France are between 8 and 12 percent, for Germany slightly more than 14 percent, and for Italy around 25 percent.[9] Venuti then connects this quantitative resistance to translations in the Anglophone world with a qualitative factor: a resistance to translations that are 'coloured' by foreignness. The dominant English and American norm has, Venuti argues, traditionally been a fluent, transparent translation which makes itself felt as little as possible, with the domestication of the foreign text, often at the cost of considerable revisions and cuts (elisions). The translator's invisibility, Venuti summarises, 'is symptomatic of a complacency in Anglo-American relations with cultural others, a complacency that can be described – without too much exaggeration – as imperialistic abroad and xenophobic at home'.[10]

If Venuti's connection between resistance to translations in general and norms of transparency should be a generally valid rule, we face a certain paradox when we turn to the situation in Sweden. In Swedish culture, the quantitative importance of translations is a generally accepted fact. As already mentioned, since the printing press came to Sweden, about half of the books published in Swedish have been translations. However, the hierarchy of source languages has varied – earlier German was dominant, this has now been replaced by English. As the writer Birgitta Trotzig said, 'translations are simply – and brutally – speaking the other

9 Lawrence Venuti, *The Translator's Invisibility. A History of Translation* (London/New York, 1995), pp. 12-14; Lawrence Venuti, *The Translator's Invisibility. A History of Translation* (London/New York, 2008), p. 11. The statistical methods used by Venuti have been questioned by scholars, including Anthony Pym in his 1999 article, 'Two Principles, One Probable Paradox and a Humble Suggestion, All Concerning Translation Rates into Various Languages, Particularly English', http://www.tinet.cat/~apym/on-line/translation/rates/rates.html, accessed June 1, 2012.

10 Venuti, *The Translator's Invisibility* (1995), op. cit., p. 17.

half of our national literature'.[11] At the same time, however, the norm of fluency and transparency, seen by Venuti as characteristic of a translation-resistant English-speaking culture, has been just as dominant in the very active Swedish translation culture as anywhere else. A low percentage of translations does thus not necessarily correlate with domestication as a norm: a fifty-fifty ratio between translations and original works in Sweden has, until recently, peacefully coexisted with invisibility.

Although Venuti's attack on the ruling Anglo-American translation ideology has not been generally accepted, it has no doubt succeeded in problematising the norm of the invisible translation and translator. In recent years, several interesting works have appeared which partly seem to correct – or are direct responses to – Venuti's generalisations of 1995. The awareness of the dynamic role of translations in Anglo-American culture was perhaps not as low as Venuti led us to believe, and is today increasing at an impressive speed. The first example of this tendency is *The Oxford Guide to Literature in English Translation*, edited by Peter France in 2000.[12] This 650 page handbook is an impressive summary of theoretical and practical knowledge about translation in the United Kingdom and the United Sstates. In it we find chapters about general problems of translation, but the greater part is devoted to descriptions of how, when, through whom and in which way, the literatures of the world have, over the centuries, reached the United Kingdom and the United States. While all of the chapters – written by 113 different specialists – meet the highest factual standards, they are also extremely readable, often entertaining, and filled with non-trivial judgements on specific translations and translators. With *The Oxford Guide to Literature in English Translation* at hand, it is difficult to say that Anglo-American literary culture is insular, imperialist and xenophobic. I do not think the book has a parallel in any other language. The impression of a high academic-level British translation history is strengthened by France's new project, *The Oxford History of Literary Translation in English*. This fundamental work will consist of five volumes, each of them the size of *The Oxford Guide*; thus far, four volumes have appeared.[13]

In a small country such as Sweden, one might wonder which conditions would have to be fulfilled for a project such as *The Oxford Guide* to be

11 Birgitta Trotzig, 'Till översättningens lov', *Dialoger* 33 (1995), p. 9.

12 Peter France, ed., *The Oxford Guide to Literature in English Translation* (Oxford, 2000).

13 Peter France and Stuart Gillespie, eds., *The Oxford History of Literary Translation in English*, vol. 1: *To 1550* (Oxford, 2008); vol. 2: *1550-1660* (Oxford, 2010); vol. 3: *1660-1790* (Oxford, 2005); vol. 4: *1790-1900* (Oxford, 2006).

undertaken – not to speak of a five-volume history of translation. However, the problem is actually not the size of the country in question. We only have to turn to Finland to find a recently published history of literary translation in Finnish, *Suomennoskirjallisuuden historia* (The History of Literary Translation in Finnish), edited by Hannu Riikonen.[14] This work, covering 450 years of translation in Finland, is also the result of an impressive collective effort. The two-volume work of about 1300 pages has involved 82 authors and has been produced in the relatively short time of six years. It is important to note that this history of translation has been published in a bilingual country. It is of course no coincidence that translation studies during the last decades have developed especially strongly – if we do not include the multicultural giants, the United Kingdom and the United Sates – in bilingual or multilingual countries such as Belgium, Canada, Finland and Israel.

How does the situation look with respect to the possibility of a history of the process by which world literature has become Swedish, and about how the Swedish language has been forced to bend and expand according to the will of foreign authors and Swedish translators? It seems that almost everything that would assist in the materialisation of a Swedish translation history is lacking. First of all, there were, until recently, few scholars working in translation studies in Sweden, and almost none were interested in the history of translation. Some work has been done on bibliographies of translations into Swedish – notably of so-called 'smaller' literatures (for example Dutch, Russian, Spanish, Portuguese and Chinese) and definitely not of translations from Anglophone literatures. Here one should specifically mention the creation of three databases: FILIS, the database for Swedish-language fiction, including translations, covering the period 1830-1900, produced at Åbo Akademi in Finland; BREFS, a bibliography of Scandinavian translations of French fiction from the same period, 1830-1900, which is a collective work based in Lund; and *Oldtidens og middelalderens litteratur i skandinaviske oversættelser* (Classic and Medieval Literature in Scandinavian Translations), which is a database for Scandinavian translations of classical and medieval literature.[15]

14 Hannu Riikonen, Urpo Kovala, Pekka Kujamäki and Outi Palaposki, eds., *Suomennoskirjallisuuden historia* 1–2 (Helsinki, 2007). Reviewed by Ritva Leppihalme in *Across Languages and Cultures* 1 (2008), pp. 139-144.

15 FILIS: http://web.abo.fi/fak/hf/sve/filis/; BREFS: http://projekt.ht.lu.se/brefs/; *Oldtidens og middelalderens litteratur i skandinaviske oversættelser*: http://skandinaviska-oversattningar.net, accessed September 1, 2012.

In the literary departments of Swedish universities there is a growing interest both in the problems of world literature and in Swedish literary history, but they almost never overlap. What Trotzig calls 'the second half' of Sweden's national literature – the translated part – still remains in the shadows. This fact – in a culture such as the Swedish, which is built on and has developed due to translations to such an extent – is not easily explained. The role of translations never seems to appear on the horizon in the many debates on how modernity conquered Sweden. Swedish culture, one has the impression, has rather wanted to be part of modernity without knowing anything about the intermediaries which brought the ideas here.

The Swedishness of Swedish literature is actually very relative, and those responsible for this relationship have to a large extent been the translators – from the Reformation Bible in the sixteenth century to the global world of today. However, this fact is not reflected in contemporary general histories of Swedish culture or Swedish literature. In a recent eight-volume cultural history of Sweden, the word *översättning*, 'translation', only appears a couple of times, and a key figure such as Hagberg is not mentioned at all.[16] In individual biographies of Swedish writers, translation is also conspicuously absent. Biographers only seem to be interested in writers creating 'original' works, rather than translations.

Actually, certain older works on the history of Swedish literature can teach us more about translations and translators than those written in recent years. To take just one important moment in Sweden's literary history – the battle over the principles of translating the Greek and Latin poets, fought at the turn of the nineteenth century between the old classicist school of paraphrase and the new 'metrical' school which was mainly inspired by German examples. This battle was perhaps not as violent as in some other countries, but in the relatively peaceful Swedish context it was heated enough.

Writing what was actually the first substantial history of Swedish literature, *Svenska Vitterheten* (Swedish belles-lettres), in 1818-1819, the critic Lorenzo Hammarsköld devoted several interesting passages to the recent debate on the principles of translation.[17] Although the main goal of

16 Jakob Christensson, ed., *Signums svenska kulturhistoria*, 1–8 (Lund/Stockholm, 2004-2009).

17 Lorenzo Hammarsköld, *Svenska vitterheten. Historiskt-kritiska anteckningar* (Stockholm, 1833).

the Romantic Hammarsköld was to describe what was *Swedish* in Swedish literature, he did not avoid the role of translations. On the contrary, in the 600 page survey of Swedish literature from the Middle Ages up to his own times, Hammarsköld devoted several pages to criticism of what he called 'the French paraphrase method' of the poet Johan Henric Kellgren (a Swedish Alexander Pope in some respects). Four pages are used to describe and quote the manifesto of the new 'metrical' school, which based its reform of verse translation, and Swedish metrics in general, on the German pre-Romantic Klopstock and the translator of Homer, Johann Heinrich Voss. The author of this manifesto, a certain Gustaf Regnér, turned against the classicist idea that Homer or Horace in translation should sound as if their texts had been written in Swedish today, which entails a complete domestication, and argued instead that one should 'find in the translation not only the ideas of the original author but also the spirit of the original language and the climate of the country, so to speak'.[18] That is, the translation should convey the foreign and the Swedish at the same time, or rather, should widen the linguistic horizon of Swedish with the help of the foreign. Although widely influential, Regnér himself was not a significant poet or translator. His Neo-Classical and Romantic principles of translation were implemented on a completely new level of poetic artistry by Gudmund Jöran Adlerbeth, whose versions of Virgil and Horace, in particular, have survived almost 200 years. Hammarsköld's *Svenska Vitterheten* devotes almost ten pages to the work of Adlerbeth.

Another work worth mentioning is *Illustrerad svensk litteraturhistoria* (Illustrated Swedish Literary History) in six volumes, by Henrik Schück and Karl Warburg, which for generations of students was *the* history of Swedish literature.[19] In this 4,000 page work from the 1920s we still find substantial information about the debate on translation at the beginning of the nineteenth century and the people who took part in it. Although they devote fewer pages to the topic than Hammarsköld's survey, we nevertheless learn quite a lot from Schück and Warburg about what one might call the post-Herderian influence on translation in Sweden at the turn of the eighteenth and the nineteenth century. Firstly, we learn

18 Gustaf Regnér, *Försök til metriske öfversättningar från forntidens skalder. Med förutgående afhandling i samma ämne* (Stockholm, 1801), p. 5.

19 Henrik Schück and Karl Warburg, eds., *Illustrerad svensk litteraturhistoria* (Stockholm, 1926-1932, ^{3}1985).

about 'humanist', that is, poetic rather than confessional translations of books of the Old Testament, secondly, 'Ossianism', that is, translations and imitations of Macpherson's *Ossian* (itself a pseudo-translation) and, finally, the new, metrical translations of the Greek and Latin classics.

If we compare Schück and Warburg with the still impressive four-volume, over 2,000 page *Ny illustrerad svensk litteraturhistoria* (New Illustrated Swedish Literary History), edited by E.N. Tigerstedt, which appeared in 1955-1957, we find significant changes.[20] Here, the watershed in Swedish translation history, the battle between the classicists and the Romantics, has been moved far into the background. The theoretician Regnér is only mentioned twice in passing, while Adlerbeth, who was an important poet and writer in his own right, is better represented, including two pages on his translations. However, the context of his practical revolution in verse translation is lost to the reader.

What is the situation for translation in the most recent multi-volume history of Swedish literature? *Den Svenska Litteraturen* (Swedish Literature), edited by Lars Lönnroth and Sven Delblanc, consists of seven volumes and comprises around 2,000 pages, but with only half as many words per page as in the two preceding histories.[21] Thus, Lönnroth and Delblanc's work is actually less than half the size of Tigerstedt's *Ny illustrerad svensk litteraturhistoria* and less than a quarter of the classic Schück and Warburg. This shortened but still comprehensive history of literature in Sweden has an explicit emphasis on sociological aspects of literature and on what the Swedish public were actually reading at a certain time. Even so, 'the second half of our national literature', the translations, high and low, classic and modern, is strikingly absent. The theoretician of foreignising translation, Regnér, is no more to be found. The great Adlerbeth receives one and a half pages, with five lines on his translations. However, the Shakespeare translator, Hagberg, who was hardly mentioned in the two earlier multi-volume works, receives one page of his own; unfortunately, the snap shot of Hagberg's versions of the Bard, which were used on Swedish stage until the end of the last century, completely lacks any contextualisation.

20 Eugène Napoleon Tigerstedt, ed., *Ny illustrerad svensk litteraturhistoria* (Stockholm, 1955-1957).

21 Lars Lönnroth and Sven Delblanc, eds., *Den svenska litteraturen* I-VII (Stockholm, 1987-1990).

The disappearance of translation history from Swedish university texts books and from the curriculum itself, when at the same time no one denies the fact that translations make up half the literature in Swedish, is not easily or quickly explained. The problem would need further research, comparison with other countries, studies on nationalism and meta-historical reflection. I can only mention a few points which I consider to be of importance in understanding the neglect of translations, translators and translation theory in Swedish literary history. Firstly, Swedish universities have never had departments for general, comparative literature, only 'literature departments', where roughly 80 percent of all research deals with literature originally written in Swedish, which mainly means, twentieth-century Swedish literature. Secondly, the notion, only lately problematised among Swedes, including politicians and intellectuals, is that 'Swedish' is basically something natural, unmarked and unproblematic, even when more languages are spoken in Sweden than ever before, and even when one-fifth of the population is considered 'immigrant', as opposed to 'native Swedish'. Finally, I want to mention the striking paradox of Swedish modernity. While eager to embrace modernity (in relation to technology, social philosophy, social sciences and the arts), at the same time, Sweden has always tended to make those who have brought modernity to Sweden invisible (immigrants, Jewish and others, translators, and migrant borderliners, even if they are of Swedish decent).

After this somewhat critical overview of the 'invisibility' of translations and translators in Sweden, I would like to turn to the description of a new database project, established at Södertörn University Library (Södertörns högskola, Huddinge, Sweden). Over the last few years a group of researchers and librarians has developed a Swedish Translators Lexicon called *Svenskt översättarlexikon*.[22] It is, in short, a database of bio-bibliographical articles about Swedish and Finland-Swedish translators from the Middle Ages to the present.

Background to the database

The new lexicon project can be said to have two sources of inspiration, one practical and one theoretical. Södertörn University has offered a

22 http://www.oversattarlexikon.se. Everyone is welcome to send comments and questions to the *Svenskt översättarlexikon* through the mailbox on our homepage.

successful Literary Translation Programme for the last fourteen years. It was a kind of Master Class series, where young translators worked on what was usually their first book under the guidance of the best literary translators in Sweden. The groups were small, usually 5-6 students, with each student attending the programme for two years on a half-time basis. Source languages included Russian, German, Polish, Finnish, French, Czech, Turkish and Estonian – all chosen in order to widen the Swedish horizons and to balance the predominance of Anglo-American literature in the book market. Regrettably, this unique programme was cancelled in 2012, for lack of financing and understanding on the part of the Vice-Chancellor; a major loss for Swedish translators, readers and book publishers. Parallel to the workshops, the Literary Translation Seminar organised lectures on the theory and history of translation.[23] In the seminar discussions about how translations are read and how the work of translators is traditionally evaluated, we found that translation criticism in Sweden – if it existed at all – traditionally meant only noting errors and making sweeping generalisations. We wondered where the positive examples were, and where we would find the description of the merits of a good translation, and of the accomplishment of individual translators. A critical bio-bibliographical lexicon of translators, who usually do not appear in existing dictionaries of writers, seemed to be the answer to these practical questions.

The theoretical inspiration for the Södertörn project was the work of the translation studies scholar, Anthony Pym. Opposing the established trend of systems-based approaches, Pym has argued that 'Humanizing Translation History' – the title of his 2008 article – is necessary. Pym says:

> ... if attention is paid to translators and only then to the texts they produce, the subjectivities thus revealed tend to display multidiscursive involvement (translators usually do more than translate), complex cultural allegiances (they are not always faithful or loyal to one side), and physical mobility (they tend not to stay in just one place).[24]

---

23 Lars Kleberg, ed., *Konsten att översätta. Föreläsningar vid Södertörns högskolas översättarseminarium 1998-2008* (Huddinge, 2008).

24 Anthony Pym, 'Humanizing Translation History', *Hermes – Journal of Language and Communication Studies* 42 (2009), p. 23, http://download2.hermes.asb.dk/archive/2009/Hermes42.html, accessed June 1, 2012.

The history of translators, Pym argues, is at least as valid an organising principle as have been the various focuses on source-text authors, source texts or target versus source languages, cultures or nations, '[o]nce you start to look at translators rather than translations, several things can be done'.[25]

Design of the database

Inspired by the discussions with our students at Södertörn and by the example of Pym, I took the initiative to start the new lexicon project. The principle for each article is simple. It consists of a comprehensive biography, a characterisation of the translator's work and its importance for its time and for today, a full bibliography of all the translator's published works, including performed but not printed scripts for plays, and a portrait of the person. By 2012 we had published the first 100 articles, thus far all about deceased translators, with the goal being closer to 1,000 articles rather than 500. The inclusion of the living and active translators, with a biography, bibliography and a portrait, is a task for the future; this work will probably be done in collaboration with the Translators' Section of the Swedish Writers Union. In addition to the bio-biographical articles published thus far, the lexicon also has other features, such as general thematic articles, the possibility to search for source languages and specific epochs, and lists of prizes awarded to translators into Swedish for the last 150 years. The use of *Svenskt översättarlexikon* is free of charge. Its further development is supported by a grant from one of the major research foundations in Sweden, Riksbankens Jubileumsfond. Our database is, to my knowledge, the only lexicon of this kind accessible to the public. However, a research group of the Slovak Academy of Sciences is preparing a lexicon of Slovak translators, both in book form and as a database. Moreover, recently, the Union of Danish Translators (a part of the Danish Authors' Society) decided to investigate the possibility of developing a Danish analogue to the Swedish lexicon. Thus, eventually we might see a network of European translators' dictionaries in progress.

The first entries in *Svenskt översättarlexikon* have already provided valuable information about Swedish and Finland-Swedish translators and their work. Every article is based on original research by linguists, literary critics, translators and librarians, and usually presents information not

25 Ibidem, p. 32.

available elsewhere. The lexicon is intended to be a source for research and eventually the basis for a history of translation in Swedish. It will then be able to help answer questions similar to those addressed by France in his introduction to *The Oxford Guide to Literature in English Translation.* What has or has not been translated into Swedish from the literatures of the world? How has translation shaped a 'canon' of world literature for Swedish readers? How have Swedish and Finland-Swedish translators seen their task, and in what social context have they worked? Under what guise have the greater and lesser works of world literature been transferred into Swedish? and What is the nature and quality of the different translations currently available to readers?[26]

Even today our database has started to serve as a reference guide for librarians, publishers and readers, and as a source for new research. This database is a step in the right direction in ensuring that a history of translation in Swedish will be completed in the future.

26 Peter France, 'Introduction', in: France, *The Oxford Guide*, p. xx.

The Reception of Scandinavian Literature in the Netherlands and Flanders 1860-1940

Some Preliminary Reflections on the Role of Networks

« Els Biesemans and Godelieve Laureys »

From the late nineteenth century onwards, interest in Scandinavian literature was on the rise throughout Europe. This is mirrored in a large number of translations of Scandinavian literary works into various European languages and is also apparent from the particular attention that Scandinavian literature received in literary journals. With reference to this sudden growth in interest across Europe, August Strindberg (1849-1919) declared to a journalist that his short plays *Playing with Fire* (*Leka med elden*) and *The Bond* (*Bandet*), both written in 1892, were translated:

> (...) from Swedish into German, from German into Italian (probably) into French which soon will be published; while the waiting English [version] will probably be translated from French as usual, after which a Swedish translation can be expected from the originally published English text.[1]

This leads Strindberg to exclaim: 'When I, in a distant future publish my Swedish originals, I will probably be accused of plagiarism'.[2]

The growing interest in Scandinavia across Europe was primarily due to the blossoming of the Scandinavian literary scene after what became

1 'från Svenskan till Tyskan, från Tyskan till Italienskan (sannolikt) till Franskan som snart utkommer; och den väntande Engelska tages sannolikt från Franskan som vanligt, hvarpå man kan vänta en Svensk öfversättning från det som Original utgifna Engelska. Utgifver jag i en aflägsen framtid mina Svenska original så blir jag sannolikt stämd för tjuftryck', Strindberg, cited in Björn Meidal, *August Strindberg. Ursvensk och europé* (Stockholm, 1999), p. 16.

2 Strindberg, cited in Meidal, *August Strindberg*, p. 16.

known as the Modern Breakthrough. The theoretical substructure of this turning point in Scandinavian literature is generally ascribed to Georg Brandes (1842-1927). This figurehead of Danish literary criticism lived in several cities in continental Europe between 1865 and 1871 in order to broaden his knowledge of the international literary scene.[3] He believed that after a long period of regurgitating literary innovations from abroad the time had come for Scandinavian literature to make a name for itself. Brandes sought to challenge the Scandinavian authors with pithy remarks such as '[o]ur literature is like a little chapel in a large church, it has its altar, but the main altar isn't to be found here'[4] and '[w]e are in fact now as always 40 years behind Europe'[5] in his *Main Currents in Nineteenth Century Literature* (*Hovedstrømninger i det 19de Aarhundredes Litteratur*). In his opinion, 'the fact that a literature in our time is lively, manifests itself in its debating of problems', and he wanted Scandinavian authors to accept the challenge to write innovative, controversial literature.[6]

The authors who shared or were influenced by Brandes' thought would soon be called 'the authors of the Modern Breakthrough'. At the turn of the century, a large number decided to move to other European cities, intending to draw on the innovative 'literature of the centre', to meet other famous literary figures and make their own names outside Scandinavia. Strindberg, for example, lived in Paris during the 1880s and 1890s, where he wrote some of his well-known novels, including *Le plaidoyer d'un fou* (*The Defence of a Fool*, 1872) and some of his prominent plays, such as *Inferno* (1897) and *Legends* (1898). As his main reason for moving away from Scandinavia was his search for a broader audience, it did not take long before he started to write in French.[7] Without doubt, Strindberg realised that international success was a necessary intermediate stage in becoming a celebrated author

3 Bertil Nolin, *Den gode europén. Studier i Georg Brandes' idéutveckling 1871-1893 med speciell hänsyn till hans förhållande till tysk, engelsk, slavisk och fransk litteratur* (Stockholm, 1965).

4 'Vor Litteratur er som et lille Kapel i en stor Kirke, den har sit Alter, men Hovedalteret findes ikke her', in: Georg Brandes, *Hovedstrømninger i det 19de aarhundredes litteratur* (Copenhagen, 1872), p. 10.

5 'Vi ere nemlig denne Gang som sædvanlig en 40 Aar tilbage for Europa', in: Brandes, *Hovedstrømninger*, p. 13.

6 'Det, at en Litteratur i vore Dage lever, viser sig i, at den sætter Problemer under Debat', in: Brandes, *Hovedstrømninger*, p. 15.

7 Meidal, *August Strindberg*, p. 24.

in his home country, where modern thought was yet to be widely accepted.[8] To emphasise this, he preferred to describe his stay abroad as an 'escape' or, more strongly, as an 'artistic exile'.[9] Henrik Ibsen (1828-1906) also chose to live abroad for the larger part of his professional life. He wrote his principal dramas *Brand* (1866) and *Peer Gynt* (1867) while in Italy and Germany between 1864 and 1891. The fact that many of his later plays, such as *Bygmester Solness* (*The Master Builder*, 1892), were first performed outside Scandinavia, illustrates the contrast between his popularity elsewhere in Europe and the lack of attention he received in his homeland.

As Scandinavian authors were actively present in other European countries, it is not so surprising that their literature received more attention. Not uncommonly, they were involved in European literary circles and acted as cultural ambassadors of a sort. Furthermore, in spite of the sometimes large distances between them, Scandinavian authors remained in close contact with each other. Many maintained a lively correspondence, discussed literary topics, commented on each other's literary works and attended performances of each other's plays. Authors such as Bjørnstjerne Bjørnson (1832-1910) and Knut Hamsun (1859-1952) even actively promoted their own country's literature abroad, thus advancing the work of their colleagues. In 1893, for example, Hamsun published an article about modern Norwegian literature, 'Le Mouvement littéraire en Norvège', in the French journal *Revue des revues*. The article received a great deal of attention, being published in the Norwegian *Morgonbladet* and the Danish *Politiken* in the same year, and a year later appearing in the German journal *Aus fremden Zungen*.[10] Bjørnson's article on modern Norwegian literature, 'Den moderne norske literatur', published in 1896, also attracted a great deal of attention. It was published in Dutch and Norwegian in the same year, and subsequently appeared in several European journals, *Zukunft* (Germany), *Tilskueren* (Denmark) and *Kringsjaa* (Norway), as well as in the American journal *Forum*.

Scandinavian literature was not disseminated solely by Scandinavian authors themselves, nor appreciated only for its intrinsic aesthetic qualities.

8 Gunnar Ahlström, *Det moderna genombrottet i Nordens litteratur* (Stockholm, 1974), p. 10.

9 Meidal, *August Strindberg*, p. 7.

10 Petra Broomans, 'Den nordiska litteraturens fälttåg i Europa kring 1900. Om Brandes och medresenärer, maktkamp och avfall', in: Olav Harsløf, ed., *Georg Brandes og Europa* (Copenhagen, 2004), p. 165.

To a certain extent, the sudden popularity of Scandinavian literature at the end of the nineteenth century can also be explained in ideological terms if we look at the ideas prevailing in the reception context. Comprehensive studies about this wider culturally oriented reception have already been conducted with respect to larger European countries such as Germany and France, but they are still lacking in relation to Flanders and the Netherlands.

An investigation of the transfer of Scandinavian literature to Flanders and the Netherlands

In order to map the reception of Scandinavian literature in these smaller language areas, a collaborative project between the University of Ghent and the University of Groningen was set up by Petra Broomans (University of Groningen) and Godelieve Laureys (University of Ghent), entitled 'The Reception of Scandinavian Literature in the Netherlands and Flanders 1860-1940. A Comparative Analysis of the Role of Networks and the Impact of the Ethnolinguistic Discourse'.[11] The project was divided into two parts, with one researcher at each university. Roald Van Elswijk (University of Groningen) concentrated on the question of the extent to which conceptions of nationalism and nationality played a role in this reception,[12] while Els Biesemans (Ghent University) focused on the roles and the social background of the transmitters who devoted themselves

11 In the project proposal, Broomans and Laureys put forward the hypothesis that in the larger European countries, Scandinavian literature was primordially perceived as 'annorlunda', i.e. 'different' and 'exotic'. One could say that this literature was received from the point of view of 'the Self', which means that its dissimilarity with the domestic literature was stressed. In the smaller European countries, however, Scandinavian literature was viewed from the perspective of 'the Other', which implies that the similarities with local literature and cultural condition were stressed. In the small language areas, moreover, the case of Scandinavian literature was put forward as evidence of how even literature written in smaller languages could be successful and in fact become well known in a context that was largely dominated by German and French literature. Thus, Scandinavian literature acquired an exemplary function and reinforced the defence of the smaller language areas' own literature.

12 More specifically, Van Elswijk focuses on the conceptualisation of 'the Other/Self'. In this part of the project, the question of how Scandinavian literature was perceived in Flanders and the Netherlands between 1860 and 1940 is addressed on the basis of a discourse analysis of reception documents.

to the promotion of Scandinavian literature to the Dutch-reading public between 1860 and 1940. This article addresses the underlying assumptions of Biesemans' research in particular.

Transmitters of literature as cultural transmitters

In contrast to the situation in France and Germany, where the Scandinavian authors themselves actively took part in the promotion of their work, in the rather peripheral Dutch language area, Scandinavian literature gained the attention of the reading public primarily through the efforts of a number of 'transmitters of literature', a phrase denoting a specific type of 'cultural transmitter'. Most transmitters of literature are translators (in this case, of Scandinavian literature into Dutch), reviewers and/or publishers but also university professors and scholars specialising in Scandinavian literature. Cultural transmitters in general also include writers of travel accounts, personal testimonies or learned essays about Nordic culture and languages, as well as scholars and librarians. It is to be noted that in many cases one and the same person fulfilled several of the above-mentioned transmission roles.[13] Although not all of them were interested in Scandinavia for the same reasons, all of these transmitters actively contributed to the increase in knowledge about Nordic culture in the Dutch language area. It is noteworthy, as previous research has indicated, that those who seem to have had much the same motives behind their interest in Scandinavian culture and literature tended to build networks and to cooperate.[14]

According to previous research related to Flanders, it is possible to discern different networks of cultural transmitters of Scandinavian culture in the late nineteenth century. In his article 'Vlaams Scandinavisme en Stijn Streuvels' (Flemish Scandinavism and Stijn Streuvels) of 1991, Diederik Grit examines adherents of the nineteenth-century Flemish Movement. Grit was able to discern three types of networks of people who showed a substantial interest in Nordic culture, labelling these networks 'the liberal

13 Petra Broomans and Marta Ronne, eds., *In the Vanguard of Cultural Transfer. Cultural Transmitters and Authors in Peripheral Literary Fields* (Groningen, 2010), p. 2.

14 Since the precise composition of the networks is still to be determined, it is not yet possible to say whether they met each other thanks to their common interest in the literature from the North, or whether they started to work with this literature because they knew each other and were influenced by each other.

national romantic circle', 'the Catholic circle' and 'the internationalist circle' respectively. Grit also noted that these circles favoured different Scandinavian authors and literary works and that different themes were emphasised in the reception of the literary works.[15] Bart Dooms was inspired by this article to further investigate the reception of Norwegian literature in Flanders. Even though Dooms, unlike Grit, did not expressly focus on the Flemish Movement as such, the study of Norwegian literature in Flanders mainly led him towards the same conclusion about the different types of networks of cultural transmission.[16]

Current studies focus on ego-networks of women and their role in the transmission of literature. Initiated by Suzan van Dijk (Huizenga Instituut/ University of Utrecht), and within the framework of the intergovernmental cooperation project *Women Writers in History*, a database of the women who engaged in transmitting literature is currently being compiled.[17] With regard to the role of networks of female translators in the reception of Scandinavian literature in particular, Ester Jiresch's (University of Groningen) forthcoming doctoral dissertation must also be mentioned.[18] Apart from their focus on women networks, the latter two research projects draw attention to the European field of cultural transmission.

One of the main objectives of our research project is to verify whether these first demarcations of the networks of cultural and literary transmitters are also applicable to a large empirical survey. Furthermore, the overview of the types of networks that were to be found in Flanders,

15 Diederik C. Grit, 'Vlaams Scandinavisme en Stijn Streuvels', *Spiegel der Letteren* 33 (3) (1991), pp. 149-170.

16 Bart Dooms, *Een gezonde noordervorst. Vlaamse visies op Noorse literatuur tussen 1830 en 1914* (Kapellen, 2001). The book is based on his Master's thesis (University of Louvain).

17 Suzan van Dijk, '"Les jugements universellement portés sur les femmes ...", Schrijfsters en lezeressen in een internationale database', *Historica*, 24 (3) (2001), pp. 3-5; Suzan van Dijk, 'Een database voor het literair-historisch onderzoek naar schrijfsters: "Women Writers before 1900"', *Muzen aan het werk. Jaarboek voor vrouwengeschiedenis* (2003), pp. 210-216; Suzan van Dijk, 'Schrijfsters vóór 1900 en hun internationale context: een database als hulpmiddel voor de geschiedschrijving', *Tijdschrift voor Genderstudies* (2003), pp. 6-15.

18 Ester Jiresch, *The Role of Networks in the Work of Female Cultural Transmitters of Scandinavian Literature and Culture in Europe around 1900. A Comparative Study of the Dutch/Flemish Side and the Austrian/German Speaking Regions* (forthcoming).

according to Grit[19] and Dooms,[20] must be supplemented by the inclusion of the situation in the Netherlands and analysed as a whole. Without anticipating the results of the thorough empirical survey that is planned, in the following the presumed situation in the Netherlands is cautiously added to the rudimentary overview of the different types of networks of Flemish cultural and literary transmitters that could be drawn on the basis of former studies.

Overview of the different types of networks

The different types of networks of transmitters of Scandinavian literature in question can be called 'the political networks', 'the ideological networks' and 'the networks of the internationalists and the modernists' respectively. The political networks can also be described as national-romantic. These networks, in particular, include exponents of the struggle of the smaller language areas for linguistic and cultural emancipation. Both Dutch and Flemish spokespeople for this struggle often referred to Scandinavia because the glorious North, with its blossoming culture and literature, was an excellent example of how even literature written in smaller languages could gain international recognition. As Scandinavian literature was regarded as an example by those interested in the development and cultivation of Dutch and Flemish culture, language and literature, within these networks special attention was paid to those Scandinavian authors who praised Nordic culture.[21] At the same time, efforts were made to emphasise the similarities between Scandinavia and the Dutch language area, both with regard to linguistic affinity and shared destiny.[22] Within these networks, there was a fervent hope that by promoting Scandinavian culture in the Dutch language area, reciprocal attention would be given to

19 Grit, 'Vlaams Scandinavisme'.

20 Dooms, *Een gezonde noordervorst.*

21 Grit, 'Vlaams Scandinavisme'; Diederik C. Grit, *Driewerf zalig Noorden: over literaire betrekkingen tussen de Nederlanden en Scandinavië* (Maastricht, 1994); Diederik C. Grit, 'Recensie: Bart Dooms, Een gezonde noordervorst. Vlaamse visies op Noorse literatuur tussen 1830 en 1914', *TijdSchrift voor Skandinavistiek* 23 (2) (2002), pp. 295-300; Margaretha Meyboom, 'Skandinavische literatuur in Nederland', *De Boekzaal* 5 (1911), pp. 45-49.

22 This search for similarities between Flemish/Dutch and Scandinavian was very often accompanied by disapproval of French literature due to its alleged depraved character and the rejection of the dominant literary language.

Dutch and Flemish literature in the Scandinavian countries. Exemplary figures within these networks are Pol de Mont and Emmanuel de Bom in Flanders, and Albert Verwey and Willem Kloos in the Netherlands.

Pol de Mont (1857-1931) by Charles Louis Philippe Zilcken (1857-1930).
Source: http://www.dbnl.org/auteurs/auteur.php?id=mont003.

Whereas in the Netherlands the specific aims of transmitting Scandinavian literature within these networks were not tied to any strong ideological views, in late-nineteenth-century Belgium the Flemish endeavours to gain recognition for the Dutch language and culture in the new kingdom added an extra dimension to the interest in Scandinavian literature. One has to keep in mind that the United Kingdom of the Netherlands, comprising the Netherlands and Belgium, came into being in 1815 under Willem I. In 1830, however, the Belgian Revolution, instigated by the French-speaking bourgeoisie, led to the creation of an independent Belgium. The constitution of the new kingdom stipulated that French was the sole official language and, consequently, all official communication was conducted in French in the new nation, in spite of the factual presence of two different language groups in the territory, the French and the Dutch. Although French was declared to be the language of the nation at the level of the 'real' state, in practice Belgium consisted of two linguistic communities. French was used in southern Belgium, while Flemish varieties of Dutch were spoken in the north, although the upper class and the ecclesiastic and juridical authorities also used French in Flanders. In the second half of the nineteenth century, an emancipation movement called De Vlaamse Beweging (The Flemish Movement) arose, aiming at gaining equal status for Flemish language and culture within the Belgian nation.[23] The fact that the veneration of Scandinavian literature in Flanders was instrumental in this Flemish movement meant that the aims of the transmission of Scandinavian literature in Flanders and the Netherlands clearly diverged.

Among the adherents of the Flemish movement, there were two different bodies of opinion, both of which were driven by a strong desire to take up positions against French cultural domination. One faction felt the urge to build a conceptual nation, the borders of which should coincide with the linguistic borders of the Dutch (including 'Flemish') language area. This group wanted to strengthen the ties with the Dutch, cherishing the idea of political restoration and dreaming of the integration of Flanders into a 'United Netherlands'. Another faction preferred Flanders to become a linguistically and culturally 'autonomous' community within the borders of the Belgian state.

This dichotomy was mirrored in the discussion about the codification of the 'Flemish' language. On the one hand, the integrationists, who believed in the idea of a 'United Netherlands', aimed at the adaptation of Flemish to the Dutch norm in the Netherlands. In addition to their wish to strengthen the alliance with the people of the Netherlands, they fostered an affinity with the speakers of other Germanic languages. The consciousness of being speakers of a minor Germanic language made them feel connected, in particular with speakers of Scandinavian languages. The unique mutual intelligibility of the Scandinavian languages was a particular case in point for integrationists such as Constant Jacob Hansen.

The particularists, on the other hand, wanted to establish a standard Flemish language distinct from the norm in the Netherlands and with its own rights within the Belgian state. For obvious reasons, the interest of the Flemish particularists in Scandinavia was specifically concentrated on the case of Norway. During the period of union with Sweden between 1814 and 1905, the issue of establishing a standard Norwegian language was omnipresent in the

23 Reginald de Schryver, 'Marie Elisabeth Belpaire', in: Reginald de Schryver et al., eds., *Nieuwe encyclopedie van de Vlaamse Beweging* (Tielt, 1998), pp. 457-458.

public debate.[24] The urban elites of Christiania (Oslo) opted for the preservation of the Norwegian language, which had been strongly influenced by Danish. The variant of the Norwegian language they favoured is today known as Bokmål. In contrast, under the impetus of Ivar Aasen, in the northwestern part of Norway the preference was for a new standard Norwegian language based on the Norwegian dialects, to be called Landsmål, later renamed Nynorsk. Flemish particularists such as Stijn Streuvels often referred to the latter in their struggle for a standard Flemish language.[25]

Apart from national-romantic considerations, the stance of the Flemish particularists was also based on religious arguments. Catholic particularists were not in favour of the idea of a 'United Netherlands' and did not want to adapt to the northern Dutch standard, mainly because of their resistance to the Calvinist dominance in the Netherlands. This also explains the existence of a second type of network with regard to the transmission of Scandinavian literature, one which was ideologically based. It is noteworthy that the adherents of this Catholic network developed a more specific interest in certain pious Scandinavian texts, in addition to their interest in the Norwegian language debate. Flemish literary transmitters belonging to this network explicitly chose to translate and review works with a religious theme. Moreover, they showed a fervent admiration for the work of the few Catholic authors, paying great attention to the work of the Dane Johannes Jørgensen (1866-1956), mainly known for his hagiographies, as well as to the Catholic Norwegian author Sigrid Undset (1882-1949). It is worth mentioning that the transmitters belonging to this network, for example Arthur Coussens, at the same time rejected the work of prominent non-Catholic authors for ethical reasons, regarding them as heretical.

Another ideologically based network found in both Flanders and the Netherlands was the network of activists within the women's liberation movement. Quite a number of well-off Dutch and Flemish women spoke other languages and naturally some became involved in translating literary texts. By explicitly selecting texts written by women or dealing with women's emancipation, women's rights within marriage or women and literature, the

24 Godelieve Laureys, 'Language Policy as a Cornerstone of Nation-Building. Linguistic Identities in the Nordic Countries', in: Petra Broomans et al., eds., *The Beloved Mothertongue. Ethnolinguistic Nationalism in Small Nations: Inventories and Reflections* (Leuven, 2008), pp. 79-91.

25 Dooms, *Een gezonde noordervorst*, p. 11.

female translators succeeded in communicating their feminist messages. As a result, famous female Scandinavian authors such as Ellen Key (1849-1892), Victoria Benedictsson (1850-1888) and Selma Lagerlöf (1858-1940) were admired and often cited as examples of female authors with international fame. With regard to the issue of women's emancipation, Scandinavia was often referred to as being 'ahead of Europe' at the time. Therefore, it should come as no surprise that Dutch and Flemish proponents of the empowerment of women explicitly chose to translate Scandinavian literature. Margaretha Meyboom (1856-1929), one of the most prominent translators of Scandinavian literature into Dutch, formulated this very clearly in an article she wrote for the journal *De Boekzaal*:

> Once we had seen how much we Dutch could learn from the Danish, the Norwegians and the Swedish with regard to social issues, the women's rights movement, handicraft and education, we seized every opportunity to emphasise this and to kindle the interest of everyone.[26]

While it may seem that the interest in Scandinavian literature in the Dutch language area arose from political or ideological convictions alone, this assumption needs to be questioned. The success of the great Scandinavian authors who created a stir on the European literary stage, such as those associated with the Modern Breakthrough, was also echoed. The transmitters of internationally admired Scandinavian literature constituted a third type of network, which can be called the network of modernists and internationalists. Within this type of network, which was particularly strong in the Netherlands, the Scandinavian authors were discussed and admired primarily because of the aesthetic qualities of their work. It must be noted, however, that the internationalists were oriented towards the literary scene in Paris and largely adopted literary tastes

26 'Toen wij eenmaal gezien hadden hoeveel wij Hollanders van Deenen, Noren en Zweden konden leeren op het gebied van sociale toestanden, vrouwenbewegingen, handenarbeid en onderwijs, namen wij elke gelegenheid waar, daar met alle nadrukt op te wijzen, en er allerwege belangstelling voor te wekken.' Meyboom, 'Skandinavische literatuur', cited in Petra Broomans, 'Scandia i Nederländerna. Om Margaretha Meijboom och hennes nordiska tidskrifter', *TijdSchrift voor Skandinavistiek* 22 (1) (2001), p. 155.

originating from there. Since the nationality of these authors who were translated and reviewed was of less importance within these networks, the fact that some of the texts were written by Scandinavian authors was not always emphasised. The fact that the members of the internationalist networks often did not translate from the original Scandinavian texts but relied on existing French and German translations also shows that they were less interested in Scandinavia as such.

Complicating and refining the picture of the networks of Dutch and Flemish transmitters of Scandinavian literature

Despite the fact that this overview of the field of transmission of Scandinavian literature in the Dutch language area offers much valuable information, it must be stressed that this framework does not do justice to the complexity of the processes of literary transmission. Empirical evidence is needed to investigate and confirm, modify or refute this framework and to gain a more balanced view of the similarities and differences between the Netherlands and Flanders. It is pertinent to question whether the boundaries between the networks mentioned above were in reality as clear-cut as earlier investigations would suggest. It is, for example, plausible that there were intersections between the networks, both with regard to the actors and to the mental legacy. Many novels by Modern Breakthrough authors, for example, received attention not only from the networks of internationalists and modernists, but also from networks of feminists. Women's position in society was a recurrent topic in the work of Bjørnstjerne Bjørnson, Henrik Ibsen, Jonas Lie (1833-1908), Erik (1846-1923) and Amalie Skram (1846-1905) and August Strindberg. In addition, the aims of the networks of the internationalists and modernists, especially in Flanders, were not always as free of nationalist sentiments as might be expected. The literary journal *Van Nu en Straks* (1893-1894 and 1896-1901), at the time regarded as modernist, should actually be characterised as 'internationally nationalistic'. Despite its strong stance against the purely linguistic concerns of the Flemish Movement, the central aspirations of this journal were indeed the consolidation of an indigenous Flemish literary life and 'the integration of Flemish art and literature into a European context'.[27] Strong testimony to this stance is apparent in a

27 Raymond Vervliet, Bart Keunen and Philippe Codde, eds., *Literatuur als woord en daad: opstellen over tekst en context in de late 19e eeuw* (Brussels, 2000), p. 93.

remarkable article, 'Vlaamsche en Europeesche Beweging' (1900) (Flemish and European Movement), by August Vermeylen (1872-1945), the editor of *Van Nu en Straks*:

> Our future depends to a large extent on the full emergence of the Flemish of Flanders. Therefore, summarised in two sentences: to become something, we have to become Flemish. – We desire to become Flemish, in order to become Europeans.[28]

As these examples suggest, some transmitters of Scandinavian literature probably acted within the scope of several networks at the same time. In his article 'Vlaams Scandinavisme en Stijn Streuvels', Diederik Grit stated that some individuals should not be thought of as belonging exclusively to one single network. Not least in this respect, the author and mediator, Stijn Streuvels, of Catholic descent but also finding himself in internationalist and modernist circles. He occupied an ambivalent, rather indefinable position. This intersection of the networks is revealed in the next section. Indeed, case studies of two key figures, examining their biographies, their contacts, the circles they moved in, their main works and their working methods, will illustrate that this ambivalence is an issue worth looking into.

Illustrative case studies

The first figure that must be mentioned with regard the period 1860-1940 is Constant Jacob Hansen (1833-1910). As early as his *Reisbrieven uit Dietschland*[29] *en Denemark* (Letters from a Journey to Germany and Denmark) of 1860, he expressed his sympathy for the idea of a 'United Netherlands' and for Pan-Germanic beliefs. Due to this ideology, he wanted to provide the Flemish with more knowledge about 'the North'. Right from the beginning he stated his goals very clearly: 'My principle purpose (...) is the encouragement of the Germanic national spirit in Flemish-Belgium, the

28 'Onze toekomst hangt grootendeels af van de grondige vervlaamsching van Vlaanderen. En daarom, in twee regels samengevat: om iets te zijn moeten wij Vlamingen zijn. – Wij willen Vlamingen zijn, om Europeërs te worden', August Vermeylen, 'Vlaamsche en Europeesche Beweging', *Van Nu en Straks* II (4) (1900), p. 299.

29 The term 'Dietsch' is a romantic denotation of the common or similar vernacular of the Low Countries. Because of a lack of a suitable English expression, this term will be used in the following.

melting together of the Flemish and the Low German language movement into one common Dietsch and powerful "struggle of the people", or in other words, the reunification of all the districts of the Low countries on a conceptual level'.[30] Of special interest to us is the fact that his anthology of Nordic literature, the first ever written in Dutch, *Noordsche Letteren* (Nordic Literature), also takes this belief as its starting point and has the same aims. This book offers many translations of poetry and plays, as well as general information about Scandinavian languages and literature. On the basis of this information, Hansen could be considered a member of the national-romantic network, being a politically active Flemish integrationist and having close contact with the other literary key figures in the Flemish Movement, Pol De Mont and Emmanuel De Bom. However, he repeatedly emphasised that he was not 'interested in political reality' and actually 'had no interest in politics'.[31] The only Pan-Germanic union he wanted to bring about was at the level of literature and language.[32]

The same wish for a cultural and linguistic unification of all people in the Dutch language area was expressed by the Dutchman Jozef A. Alberdingk Thijm, who chose the title *De Dietsche Warande* for the journal he established in 1855. From the beginning, the target group of this journal were Catholics in the predominantly Calvinist Netherlands. When the interest of this target group turned out to be rather weak, the editorship of the journal was handed over to Jozef Alberdingk Thijm's brother, Paul Alberdingk Thijm, who at the time was a professor at the University of Louvain in Belgium. Although Catholicism in Flanders is traditionally linked with particularist thought, he explicitly warned against all forms of particularism or provincialism in his 1886 article 'Een woord van eendracht' (A word of concord) in the Flemish journal *Het Belfort*.

30 'Mijn Hoofddoel (...) is in Kortbegrip: de Opwekking, in breederen Sin, des germaanschen Volksgeestes in Vlaamsch-Belgien, de Versmelting der vlaamsche met der platduitsche Taalbeweging tot eenen algemeen dietschen en machtigen Volkskamp, oft de Hereeniging aller nederduitsche Gewesten op geestelyken Gebiede', Constant Jacob Hansen, *Reisbrieven uit Dietschland en Denemark* (Ghent, 1860), p. 1.

31 Alex Bolckmans, *From Nordic Folk Tales to Science Fiction* (Ghent, 1988), p. 17.

32 Ludo Simons, 'Vlaams-Nederduitse betrekkingen in de 19e eeuw', in: Ludo Simons, *Oostnoordoost. Facetten van de uitstraling van Vlaanderens taal en literatuur* (Antwerp, 1969), p. 29.

Jozef Albertus Alberdingk Thijm (1820-1889).
To an engraving by P.J. Arendzen, Atlas van Stolk (Rotterdam).
http://www.dbnl.org/tekst/dong001dier01_01/dong001dier01_01_0009.php.

In 1900, both *De Dietsche Warande* and *Het Belfort* were taken over by the Flemish literary critic Marie-Elisabeth Belpaire (1853-1948), and the resulting integrated journal was named *Dietsche Warande en Belfort.*

Dietsche Warande en Belfort.

Belpaire was also strongly influenced by her Catholic beliefs, but she did not regard particularism or provincialism as a threat. On the contrary, in the article 'Boekennieuws. J. Destrée over het talenvraagstuk in België' (News about Books. J. Destrée on the language question in Belgium), published in *Dietsche Warande en Belfort* in 1924, Belpaire even referred to the above-mentioned Danish author Johannes Jørgensen's 'Klokke Roeland', as a true glorification of Flanders, clarifying her particularist stance. This was not the only article in which Belpaire expressed feelings of Flemish self-awareness. Furthermore, she generally disapproved of the work of internationally praised modernist authors, preferring instead works with religious themes. She, of course, saw to it that these preferences were mirrored in *Dietsche Warande en Belfort.* Not surprisingly, this journal paid a great deal of attention to Jørgensen, one of Belpaire's favourite authors. Nonetheless, the work of the Norwegian Modern Breakthrough author Bjørnstjerne Bjørnson was also appreciated, not because of the modernist bias of his work, of course, but rather because of the pure, unspoiled and pious character of the people portrayed in his peasant novels. She also praised the portrayal of the romantic-national character of the people in the works of both Bjørnson and Jørgensen. The picture is even more complicated in view of the efforts of Belpaire concerning the emancipation of women, though to a certain extent, these efforts could be explained as resulting from the will to offer young women a dignified, Catholic education.[33] Finally, Belpaire's contacts with and admiration of some passionate, atheist feminists shows the difficulties of classifying her into one single network.

Marie-Elisabeth Belpaire in her study, 1934. From Collection AMVC-Letterenhuis, Antwerp.

Concluding remarks and further stepping stones

It seems to be a challenging enterprise to give a general description of the reception of Scandinavian literature and map the networks of Dutch and Flemish transmitters of Scandinavian literature between 1860 and 1940. However informative, the tentative network model presented in this article does not fully correspond to nor reflect the complexity of the actual

33 Ester Jiresch, 'Marie-Elisabeth Belpaire and Dina Logeman-Van der Willigen: Two cultural transmitters in Flanders - in the Same literary Field?', in: Broomans and Ronne, *In the Vanguard*, pp. 33-54; De Schryver, 'Marie Elisabeth Belpaire', pp. 457-458.

processes of literary transmission. The main issue is that the demarcations between the networks of literary transmitters described by previous research are in reality not as clear-cut as suggested.

When aiming to establish a more nuanced view of the constitution of the field of literary transmission, a comprehensive study including every transmitter of Scandinavian literature into the Dutch area seems necessary. This can be achieved by constructing a prosopography, which is a thorough method for studying cultural history starting from historical figures, in this case the literary transmitters of Scandinavian literature to the Dutch language area. For all of the literary transmitters included in the research population, a parallel set of data about their social lives, mutual relationships, educational backgrounds, publication patterns and other indicators of their reputation, position and centrality with respect to the transmission of Scandinavian literature to the Dutch language area should be collected. This implies the efficient collection and thorough examination of the reception documents, critical reviews, translations, journal articles, letters and other ego-documents originating with each transmitter, as well as a collection of the texts referring to the transmitters concerned.

By setting up a prosopography based on this data, the structure of the population of literary transmitters can be examined and recurrent patterns regarding their transmitting behaviour unveiled.[34] In view of storing the prosopographical data in a way that makes it fully accessible for further research, a relational database is being created. The sets of data in the base can be approached from different angles with the help of extended search functions and programs for geometric data analysis. Thus, certain patterns and evolutions can be established and the different mechanisms underlying the transfer of Scandinavian literature to the Dutch language area can be investigated and discerned. After analysing, combining and interpreting the prosopographical data, a better understanding of how these literary transmitters are actually related to each other will be established. Finally, the tentative network model outlined in this paper will then be able to be tested against the findings of such prosopographical analysis.

34 Koenraad Verboven, Myriam Carlier and Jan Dumulyn, 'A Short Manual to the Art of Prosopography', in: Katharine Keats-Rohan, ed., *Prosopography Approaches and Applications. A Handbook* (Oxford, 2007), p. 60.

Peripheral Autonomy/Mutual Sympathy?

Women Translators in Flanders, 1870-1914[1]

« Liselotte Vandenbussche »

What are the various motives of women writers from peripheral literary fields in choosing particular authors or works for translation? Is it a shared feeling of remoteness from the literary centre that inspires them to bond? Does their social, educational or economic capital play a decisive role? Are there more ideological or selfish motives involved, such as the formation of a canon or the search for prestige? Or is it all just a matter of pure coincidence?

The following provides a short sketch of the – relatively small – importation of foreign literature by women translators in Flanders between 1870-1914, focusing on the various source literatures and kinds of imports. The chosen starting point is 1870, a time when a literary awakening in Flanders was slowly but steadily occurring. The *terminus ad quem* for this research is 1914, when the First World War shook the foundations of the cultural world.

This research is based on my doctoral thesis on liberal and anarchist women writers in Flanders.[2] I focus on women, partly to make the research feasible, as material was largely available, singling out a fairly limited group compared to all Flemish translators that were active in 1870-1914, and partly because research has shown that it was often women who took up translation as a profession.[3]

1 This article is a revised version of Liselotte Vandenbussche, 'The Import of English Literature by Women Translators in Flanders, 1870-1914. A Comparative Survey', in: Tom Toremans and Walter Verschueren, eds., *Crossing Cultures. Nineteenth-Century Anglophone Literature in the Low Countries* (Leuven, 2009), pp. 137-154.

2 Liselotte Vandenbussche, *Het veld der verbeelding. Vrijzinnige vrouwen in Vlaamse literaire en algemeen-culturele tijdschriften (1870-1914)* (Ghent, 2008).

3 Marysa Demoor, *Their Fair Share. Women, Power and Criticism in the Atheneum, from Millicent Garett Fawcett to Katherine Mansfield, 1870-1920* (Aldershot, 2000); Louise von Flotow, *Translation and Gender. Translating in the 'Era of Feminism'* (Manchester/Ottowa, 1997); Isabelle Kalinowski, 'La vocation au travail de la traduction', *Actes de la recherche en sciences sociales* 144 (3) (2002), pp. 47-54.

The term 'translator' is used here because these women did not all act as 'cultural transmitters' in the sense that they 'searched actively for literature abroad, contacting the authors in many cases'.[4] Only Dina Logeman-van der Willigen can be labelled as such, while Virginie Loveling conforms to the more elaborate definition of someone who 'takes on various roles in the field of cultural transmission: translator, reviewer, critic, journalist, [...], editor of a journal, writer, travel writer'.[5]

I will supplement this overview with some background information on the secondary schooling and higher education of women in Flanders and other elements that played a role in the translation market. Pierre Bourdieu's theory of the literary field and Rakefet Sela-Sheffy's supplement to it will act as guidelines in this research. Special focus will lie on the wide-ranging motives of women translators, whether it was to earn money, to spread ideas and influence the reading public, or consolidate or prefigure an existing or future literary repertoire. This will result in a qualitative micro-study that does not regard translations from a publisher's point of view,[6] but approaches the work from the perspective of the translators themselves.

This analysis does not include a quantitative comparison of the production of translations, since that would mean including translations by male authors as well, which would greatly exceed the scope of this

4 Jaap Grave, *Zulk vertalen is een werk van liefde. Bemiddelaars van Nederlandstalige literatuur in Duitsland 1890-1914* (Nijmegen, 2001), p. 13.

5 For a discussion of Logeman-van der Willigen as a cultural transmitter, see Ester Jiresh, 'Marie-Elisabeth Belpaire and Dina Logeman-Van der Willigen. Two Cultural Transmitters in Flanders – in the Same Literary Field?', in: Petra Broomans and Marta Ronne, eds., *In the Vanguard of Cultural Transfer. Cultural Transmitters and Authors in Peripheral Literary Fields* (Groningen, 2010), pp. 33-54. For a discussion of Loveling as a cultural transmitter, see Liselotte Vandenbussche, Griet Vandermassen, Marysa Demoor and Johan Braeckman, 'Virginie Loveling (1836-1923) as a Cultural Mediator: From Translating Klaus Groth to Manipulating Charles Darwin', in: Petra Broomans, ed., *From Darwin to Weil. Women as Transmitters of Ideas* (Groningen, 2009), pp. 47-71. For an elaborate definition of a 'cultural transmitter', see Petra Broomans, 'Introduction: Women as Transmitters of Ideas', in: Broomans, *From Darwin to Weil*, p. 2.

6 For an example of such an approach see Adriaan van der Weel, 'Nineteenth-Century Literary Translations from English from a Book Historical Context', in: Martine de Clercq, Tom Toremans and Walter Verschueren, eds., *Textual Mobility and Cultural Transmission = Tekstmobiliteit en culturele overdracht* (Leuven, 2006), pp. 27-40.

article. Instead, the analysis will focus on some of the reasons why women writers chose translation in general, or specific authors and source literatures in particular.[7]

Source Literatures

When looking at the source literatures that women chose or were asked to translate, some tendencies become clearly visible. A quick overview of the works translated by women during the late nineteenth and early twentieth centuries in Flanders shows us that they mainly chose authors from the German, Danish, Norwegian and Swedish literary systems. English and French works, as well as Russian, Estonian and Greek, were rarely chosen for translation.

Scandinavian Literatures

When looking at the number of translations, works from the smaller Danish, Norwegian and Swedish communities clearly outnumber all other source systems. This is mainly due to the huge number of translations by Dina Logeman-van der Willigen (1864-1925), a Dutch professional translator living in the Belgian city of Ghent, who published more than one hundred translated novels by the Danish writers Jørgensen, Brandes and Bang, and the Swedish author Key.[8] Apart from Logeman-van der Willigen, Marie-Elisabeth Belpaire (1853-1948), the founder and editor of

7 The results are partly based on my PhD research on the contribution of liberal women writers to cultural magazines and literary journals between 1870 and 1914: *Het veld der verbeelding. Het aandeel en de receptie van niet-confessionele publicistes in Vlaamse, literaire en algemeen-culturele tijdschriften, 1870-1914*. By finding their contributions and analysing their correspondence, I gained a fairly detailed view of the women writers who translated poetry and prose. To that information, I also added data from secondary sources and library catalogues.

8 Dina Logeman-van der Willigen published translations of the following authors: Hans Aanrud, Herman Bang, Jenny Blicher-Clausen, Johan Bojer, Walter Christmas, Elsa Dovlette-Lindberg, Carl Ewald, Evy Fogelberg, Christian Gierloeff, Per Hallström, Rakel Harbitz, Verner von Heidenstam, Frank Heller, Adolf Johansson, Johannes Jørgensen, Aho Juhani, Ellen Key, Bernt Lie, Johannes Linnankoski, Sophus Michaëlis, Avilde Prydz, Barbra Ring, Ingeborg Maria Sick, Werner Söderhjelm, R. Steffen, Marieke Stjernstedt, Sigrid Undset. They were all published by Dutch houses, with Belgian houses publishing only a few translations.

the Catholic literary and cultural journal *Dietsche Warande en Belfort*, also translated some of Jørgensen's works. In addition, the unknown Mathilda van Engelen adapted a Scandinavian fairy tale, and Virginie Loveling (1836-1923) translated a poem by Knut Hamsun, which was published in a review of modern Norwegian literature by Logeman-van der Willigen in 1908.[9]

Dina Logeman-van der Willigen, March 1923. University Library Ghent.

German Literatures

For most women translators German literature functioned as a source system. The sisters Paula and Mina Sleeckx (1871-1938) and Rosalie and Virginie Loveling, as well as Laura Hiel (1859-1945), Esther Stinissen, Siska van Daelen (1879-1944) and Hélène Swarth (1859-1943) published work by authors such as Victor Blüthgen, Paul Heyse and Eugenie Marlitt, the Austrian writer Emil(e) Mario Vacano, as well as Klaus Groth, Heinrich Heine, August von Platen, the unknown Katharina Koch and Emil Schattke, and the Romanian princess Carmen Sylva (Elisabeth Pauline Ottilie Luise zu Wied).

English Literatures

During the late nineteenth and early twentieth centuries only a small number of translations of English works were done by women translators.

9 Loveling's translation of Knut Hamsun's poem 'Munken Vendt' is found on pages 81-82 of the review.

They were all writers themselves, producing one or more translations as a sort of side project to their own creative work. They include Maria van Ackere-Doolaeghe (1803-1884), Siska Van Daelen, Hélène Swarth and Anna Germonprez (1866-1957). The British and Scottish authors whose works were translated were Henry Wadsworth Longfellow, Lord Byron, John Henry Mackay, Elizabeth Barrett Browning, Oscar Wilde and Ian Maclaren (John Watson). The origins of these translations can be documented by means of the translators' correspondence.

In 1878, Van Ackere-Doolaeghe asked Eugène van Oye (1840-1926), a poet who had published translations of Longfellow and William C. Bryant, if he was willing to revise her translation of a poem by Lord Byron.[10] Given that she did not have a command of English, Van Ackere-Doolaeghe confessed, she had asked a friend to translate it into French, which she had, in turn, translated into Dutch. As was often the case in France, the translation had been a joint effort.[11] Because her friend could not read Dutch and was therefore unable to make a judgement about the Dutch translation, she asked Van Oye to revise her work. Thanking him for his translation of the poem, which she would use as an aid to rewrite her work, she added her translation creed, borrowed from Abbé Delettre: 'The most essential duty of a translator, which implies everything else, is to try to make the same effort as the author in every part of the work'.[12]

Germonprez, a teacher and writer, was asked to translate a literary work by the Scottish writer Ian Maclaren by her friend Belpaire. The latter had just published a study on Maclaren in May 1900 and wanted to provide her readers with a translation of his work.[13] Germonprez, who had shown a fondness for Flemish traditions and knowledge of the Flemish national character in her novels, seemed to be tailor-made for the job and at first agreed. She liked

10 Maria van Ackere-Doolaeghe to Eugeen Van Oye, January 2, 1875, University Library Ghent, Hs 3375, no. 165.

11 Blaise Wilfert, 'Cosmopolis et l'homme invisible. Les importateurs de littérature étrangère en France, 1885-1914', *Actes de la recherche en sciences sociales* 144 (2002), pp. 36-37.

12 'Le devoir le plus essentiel du traducteur, celui qui les renferme tous, c'est de chercher à produire dans chaque morceau le même effort que son auteur.'

13 Geraldine Reymenants, *Vrouweninvloed in het literaire veld. De medewerking van vrouwen aan katholieke Vlaamse tijdschriften, weekbladen en kranten* (Ghent, 2005), p. 113.

Beside the Bonnie Brier Bush, 'so tolerant, uplifting, stimulating the good'.[14] However, the translation did not turn out to be that easy. The religious situation in the novel was typically Scottish and, according to Germonprez, difficult to explain to 'our nation'. Moreover, the Scottish dialect of the peasants would not be convincing when translated into her own dialect.[15] When the work was finally published in *Dietsche Warande en Belfort*, Germonprez used the typical strategy of the 'humble servant', revealing her concern and almost apologising to a colleague who had made some remarks; she emphasised that the translation was made at the insistence of Belpaire and that translating was not one of her best qualities.[16]

Romance Literatures

Almost no works by French-speaking authors in Belgium or writers from France, Italy or Spain were translated. Exceptions to this rule were Van Ackere-Doolaeghe, who translated a French poem by the Belgian Minister of State, Rogier, in 1872 ('De tehuiskomst'), and Swarth, who translated work by Charles Fuster ('Een doode') in 1888 and, after her move to the Netherlands in 1894, work by Johannes Allarda, Alfred de Musset and Rachilde (Marguerite Vallette-Eymery). These findings confirm the general situation taking male translators into account, with only one-fifth of all translations into Dutch (1830-1914) being translated from French.[17] The largest group (one-third) consists of translations from German, with French being followed by English and smaller languages.

The reasons for this relative lack of interest could be manifold. A first and obvious reason is that the intellectual elite and most literate people spoke and read French in Belgium and therefore did not need translations. It also points to the centrality of French literature in the cultural world-system.[18] A second reason, however, might be that in Flanders, French

14 Ibidem, p. 114: 'zoo verdraagzaam, verheffend, tot zedelijk groote zaken opwekkend'; Anna Germonprez to Marie-Elisabeth Belpaire, June 15, 1900, AMVC, B417/B2, no. 80751/10.

15 Anna Germonprez to Marie-Elisabeth Belpaire, June 15, 1900 and December 22, 1900, AMVC, B417/B2, no. 80751/7.

16 Anna Germonprez to Alfons de Cock, January 10, 1902, AMVC, G314/B1, no. 13394/401.

17 Liselotte Vandenbussche, 'Towards a cartography of intracultural relations in Belgium (1830-1914)'. Unpublished paper presented at the international colloquium 'Translation in multilingual cultures', Leuven, May 20-22, 2009.

18 Johan Heilbron, 'Het wereldvertaalstelsel', *Filter* 7 (2000), p. 43.

literature had long been regarded as dandyish and perverse, in contrast to a sound and healthy literature.[19] The critic Frans de Potter (1834-1904), for instance, was clearly delighted with Rosalie Loveling's (1834-1875) 1864 translation of a novel by the German writer Klaus Groth (1819-1899) and placed the work in sharp contrast with the 'light literature' of the South.[20]

Other Peripheral Literatures

Russia, Romania, Estonia and Greece sporadically functioned as source systems for women translators in Flanders, but in most of these translations the original authors were not mentioned and are thus difficult to identify. Only Laura Hiel's (1859-1945) 1895 translation of Turgenev and Swarth's 1909 translation of Hélène Vacaresco explicitly mention the original authors. Those translations published without a reference to the author were probably not directly translated from the original. Mina Sleeckx's (1851-1939) Slavonic fairy tales, for example, were translated from Marmier's *Contes populaires de différents pays.* Also, in the case of translations of folktales from Turkish and Hebrew no source was mentioned and it seems unlikely that they would have been translated from the original sources.

Kinds of Import

Using Blaise Wilfert's continuum of practices,[21] we can observe that the most prestigious forms associated with literary import, such as prefaces, conferences, chronicles and criticism, were not widely used by these women translators. Only Logeman-van der Willigen and Belpaire seem to use their participation in literary journals as a conscious means of stimulating interest in their translations. Virginie Loveling looked for a position as a chronicler during the early 1880s but never succeeded in obtaining such a position. She wrote one review on Groth (1881) in which she stressed the excellent quality of his work, yet never explicitly presented him as the promise for the future of literature in Flanders. Van Ackere-Doolaeghe

19 Jean-Marie Klinkenberg, 'De Franse literatuur in Vlaanderen', in: Mathieu Rutten and Jean Weisgerber, eds., *Van Arm Vlaanderen tot De voorstad groeit* (Antwerp, 1988), p. 519.

20 Ludo Simons, *Vlaamse en Nederduitse literatuur in de 19de eeuw. II. Vertalingen, receptie, beïnvloeding* (Ghent, 1985), p. 336.

21 Wilfert, 'Cosmopolis et l'homme invisible', pp. 35-36.

wrote a foreword to the translation of Rogier's poem and Swarth published some reviews and prefaces in which she included her views on authors she had translated. Most of the other women merely published the translations themselves, without any secondary or commentary supplements such as essays or literary criticism in journals.

Prose translations were by far the most prominent. Hiel, Virginie Loveling, Lava, Mina Sleeckx and Germonprez mainly published short stories and novellas. Mina Sleeckx and Mathilda van Engelen translated or adapted fairy tales. Poetry was mainly translated by women who wrote poetry themselves, such as Van Ackere-Doolaeghe, Hiel, Swarth and Van Daelen. Their publications appeared both in cultural magazines and literary journals, as well as in separate volumes. The journals in which they published were fairly traditional and conservative institutions, although the translated authors were sometimes considered progressive writers in their homeland, such as the decadent writer Herman Bang in Denmark. They did not include *petites revues* in which experimentation was encouraged. Logeman-van der Willigen and Swarth also published their translations in book form. Some of the translations mentioned above were first published in journals and later distributed as separate works, such as that of Virginie Loveling and Germonprez.

Linguistic Proficiency and Educational Resources

Most of these women translators excelled in several languages. Their family resources came in handy, since they often could not rely on other resources such as schooling. Secondary schools for girls which offered a quality education in Dutch were rare in Flanders before the last quarter of the nineteenth century. In addition to Catholic and private institutions that offered only a limited curriculum (catechism, reading, sometimes writing and arithmetic, French, housekeeping, but above all embroidering, sewing, dancing and painting), the first municipal secondary school for girls was only founded in Brussels in 1864 by the feminist Isabelle Gatti de Gamond (1839-1905).[22] It aimed for higher standards in education and offered natural sciences rather than religion.[23]

22 Marijke Verbeke, *Rijksmiddelbaar onderwijs voor meisjes: 100 jaar geleden een werkelijkheid* (Ghent, 1982), p. 5.

23 Ibidem, p. 24.

Apart from twenty-five municipal initiatives inspired by Gatti de Gamond's example,[24] it was not until 1881 that a law was enacted which provided for fifty lower secondary schools for 11 to 15-year-old girls. This measure still stands in contrast to the hundred secondary schools provided for boys, supplementing the state initiatives taken since the 1850s, where boys from the higher classes received six to seven years of secondary schooling, with two to four hours of English in the last four to five years, Dutch and French over seven years, and Greek and Latin for five or six years.[25] German was only introduced in 1879.[26] In theory, girls were to have the same school curriculum as boys in lower secondary school,[27] but in practice they had fewer classes in Dutch, French and German, and, remarkably, more classes in English.[28] This changed quickly and in 1888 the three hours of German and English in lower secondary school became optional.[29] In 1897, girls received two hours of English and German in their second and third years of vocational education.[30] English and German in the more general curriculum remained optional.

In the Netherlands, the situation was different. Qualitative secondary state education in Dutch was provided much earlier to both boys and girls, and girls had more opportunity to study languages.[31] Moreover, the secondary school final exam contained, for example, translations of prose or elementary poetry from French, German and English.[32] It might explain Logeman-van der Willigen's complaint that proficiency in English was so widespread that translating English works was not lucrative for her.

Finally, there were also teachers' training colleges in Belgium. In 1849, ten state institutions instructed prospective schoolmistresses for primary schools,[33] while in 1879 and 1880 colleges were founded in Liège and Brussels to train secondary school teachers for the newly established state

24 Ibidem, p. 56.

25 Martin Brants, *De hervorming van het middelbaar onderwijs* (Ghent, 1906), pp. 25-26.

26 Ibidem, p. 27.

27 Ibidem, p. 53.

28 Verbeke, *Rijksmiddelbaar onderwijs voor meisjes*, p. 47.

29 Brants, *De hervorming van het middelbaar onderwijs*, p. 54; Verbeke, *Rijksmiddelbaar onderwijs voor meisjes*, pp. 49-50.

30 Brants, *De hervorming van het middelbaar onderwijs*, p. 61.

31 Ibidem, pp. 106-107.

32 Ibidem, pp. 103-105.

33 Verbeke, *Rijksmiddelbaar onderwijs voor meisjes*, p. 23.

institutions.[34] These schools offered the only form of higher education available to 15-year-old girls and lasted two years. They had science and literature streams, where English and German were optional, and a modern languages stream, where four languages were compulsory. At the end of 1912, the course of study was prolonged to three years.[35] In the primary school teachers' colleges, English and German were taught as optional third languages.[36]

Some of the women mentioned above had undertaken such education, others were teaching in the schools themselves. Mina Sleeckx taught Dutch, English and German in a state college for women teachers in Liège, while Paula Sleeckx was the head of such a college in Bruges. Anna Germonprez, Fanny Delvaux and Laura Hiel taught at primary schools. Germonprez also spent some years studying in Great Britain and Germany, living in Herne Bay (Kent) for more than two years and spending eighteen months in Hof (Bavaria).[37]

The other women mentioned did not attend secondary school or teachers' college and had to rely on their family resources and travel experiences. The Loveling sisters' father was German and he knew the main European languages, reading many authors in the original language.[38] He taught his daughters German at an early age,[39] in addition to the French and Dutch they spoke at home. Using their father's grammar books and dictionaries after his death, the sisters taught themselves English, Italian and Spanish, as well as Danish and Swedish. In her diary, Virginie Loveling writes that they spoke a different language every day from morning until noon. She made some trips to visit friends in Britain and Australia and presumably had a good command of English.

34 Ibidem, p. 26.

35 Inge Alliet and Isabelle Deridder, *Geschiedenis van de wetgeving in verband met het middelbaar onderwijs voor meisjes (1894-1962). Casus middelbare normaalschool Onze-Lieve-Vrouw-ten-Doorn Eeklo* (Master's thesis Ghent University, 2005), p. 46.

36 *Programmes de l'enseignement à donner dans les écoles normales et les sections normales primaires de l'état* (Ghent, 1892), pp. 40-43.

37 Edgard Rijckaerts, *Jeronimo: verzamelde novellen door Anna Germonprez; met voorrede en levensschets van de schrijfster* (Antwerp, 1950), pp. 14, 239.

38 Virginie Loveling to Paul Fredericq, May 8, 1914, University Library Ghent, Hs III 69, p. 178.

39 Antonin van Elslander and Anne Marie Musschoot, 'Correspondentie van de Gezusters Loveling. Brieven van en aan Paul Fredericq II', *Mededelingen van het Cyriel Buysse Genootschap* 10 (1994), pp. 19-20.

Hélène Swarth was raised in Brussels and learnt French at boarding school.[40] Her father taught her German and she taught herself English, probably from written sources only. She read and understood the latter almost perfectly but was not capable of speaking it very fluently. She wrote her debut work in French but switched to Dutch in the early 1880s.

Logeman-van der Willigen went to Denmark and learnt Danish afterwards to be able to read Andersen's fairy tales. She also later learnt Swedish and translated Finnish works using Swedish intertexts.[41] Her husband, Henri Logeman (1862-1936), was a professor of Dutch linguistics who later founded the Scandinavian Department at Ghent University and joined his wife on her many journeys to the North.

Fanny Lava (1858-1938), also known as Florence MacLeod-Maertens, was a friend of Peter and Sophie Kropotkin. She translated non-fictional works by Kropotkin from Russian into English in 1904 and 1907, for which she was highly praised.[42] Unfortunately a broader network of international or Russian contacts could not be traced. Lava probably relied on her husband's income, which gave her enough time to invest in language acquisition, such as learning Russian. Her letters are kept in the Uppsala University Library and include many from and to her Russian friends.

Money as a Motive

The reasons why these women started to translate were often mundane. Many of them mention in their letters that they mainly translated to earn some extra money. Logeman-van der Willigen, for whom translating was an important source of income, since her husband was often ill,[43] even let money decide what kind of literature she translated. The fierce competition from many young women who were able to translate from English and were apparently willing to do it at very low prices made her opt for the more 'exotic' and unfamiliar Scandinavian languages. In December 1913 she wrote to her friend Belpaire: 'I never translate works from English because

40 Hélène Swarth to Lode Scheltjens, June 29, 1938, AMVC S995/B, no. 19754/5.

41 Petra Broomans, '"Vertalingen waar haast bij is, boeken die gerecenseerd moeten worden". Dien Logeman-Van der Willigen', *Spieghel Historiael* 42 (2002), p. 50.

42 Paul Hamelius, 'Boekbeoordeling', *Vlaanderen* 2 (1904), p. 486.

43 Dina Logeman-van der Willigen to Marie-Elisabeth Belpaire, October 16, 1912, AMVC-Letterenhuis, B417/B2, no. 166196/2438a-c, 2439.

it *does not pay*. Everyone in Holland is able to translate from English [and] publishers are flooded by requests from young girls who want to translate a *whole* book for 5 or 10 guilders!!'[44]

Rather than choosing British authors, Logeman-van der Willigen opted for writers from the smaller Danish, Norwegian and Swedish communities, such as Johannes Jørgensen, Georg Brandes, Ellen Key and Herman Bang.[45] By selecting these authors for her Dutch translations she was not only able to satisfy a demand for highbrow literature from the then popular Scandinavian countries, but also managed to earn a living from her translations, which might well have been impossible if she had focused on English or French literature. In addition to the highbrow literature, Logeman-van der Willigen also translated lowbrow literature, for example novels by Jenny Blicher-Clausen, who enjoyed immense popularity at the time. Her fellow-translator Margaretha Meyboom did not support this change of direction and attempted to promote only highbrow literature.[46]

Virginie Loveling was not paid for the translations of German, English and Swedish texts that she published before 1870. She did not seem to mind, considering it a nice occupation and a good exercise.[47] However, when she moved to Ghent to live on her own, the need for money became an important motive to publish. In 1880, she wanted a job that would yield both intellectual satisfaction and a regular income. She longed to earn some money as a correspondent for a journal abroad by providing translations and summaries, or by joining the editorial board of a periodical.[48] She preferred to translate non-fictional work, stating that '[i]f it is not a work of imagination, which is really difficult to render into a foreign language, it goes very well'.[49] In a letter to her nephew Paul Fredericq, she wrote: 'I'd

44 'Ik vertaal nooit uit het Eng. omdat het zich niet betaalt. Iedereen in Holland kan uit het Eng. vertalen + de uitgevers worden overstroomd door jonge meisjes die voor 5 of 10 gulden een heel boek willen vertalen!!', Dina Logeman-van der Willigen to Marie-Elisabeth Belpaire, December 1913, AMVC-Letterenhuis, B417/B2, no. 166169/2442.

45 See Broomans, 'Vertalingen waar haast bij is'.

46 Broomans and Ronne, *In the Vanguard of Cultural Transfer*, p. 3.

47 Virginie Loveling to Maurits Basse, s.d., University Library Ghent, Nalatenschap Maurits Basse, Hs III 69, pp. 350-351.

48 Virginie Loveling to Paul and Leon Fredericq, February 4, 1880, Van Elslander and Musschoot, 'Correspondentie van de Gezusters Loveling', pp. 41-42.

49 Ibidem.

prefer to make summaries for the *Athenaeum belge*. That and translations, I consider – between you and me – to be my specialty'.[50]

Nonetheless, she had ambivalent feelings about translating prose. She wrote, again to her cousin and counsellor: 'For the moment, I am working on a translation of "Witen Kross" by Klaus Groth. It is very difficult, but extremely enjoyable. It is – so to say – only *main d'oeuvre*'.[51] In 1882, she wrote again to Fredericq: 'I cannot always write original work and I am looking for an occupation: if you could find me something to translate or review I would be most grateful'.[52] However, the difficulties and small sums for translating fiction and non-fiction ultimately meant she had to rely on her own children's stories, folklore, literary reports and, of course, novels to earn a decent living. The translation of a poem by Knut Hamsun in 1908 was her last, and was probably done at the insistence of Logeman-van der Willigen.

Hélène Swarth also had an ambivalent view about translating. She saw it as a 'humble' option in comparison to her other creative work.[53] Since she could not live decently from the money she earned by publishing poetry, she felt obliged to turn to prose, children's literature and translations, which she often regarded as drudgery. In 1882, she asked a Dutch publisher for permission to translate a work by the British writer Ouida.[54] In 1887, she wrote to her colleague Pol de Mont (1857-1931): 'Just a word to ask if you know a publisher who pays rather well for translations. I have put

50 'Liefst zou ik résumés voor het Ath. B. maken, *dat* en vertalingen aanzie ik, onder ons gezeid, voor mijne specialiteit', Virginie Loveling to Paul Fredericq, October 24, 1880, Van Elslander and Musschoot, 'Correspondentie van de Gezusters Loveling', p. 58.

51 'Thans werk ik aan eene vertaling van 'Witen Kross' van Klaus Groth. Zeer moeilijk, doch dat doe ik buitengewoon gaarne, het is toch om zoo te zeggen maar main d'oeuvre', Virginie Loveling to Paul Fredericq, January 19, 1881, Van Elslander and Musschoot, 'Correspondentie van de Gezusters Loveling', p. 68.

52 'Ik kan niet altijd oorspronkelijke stukken schrijven en zoek bezigheid, indien gij mij iets te vertalen of te critikeeren kondet aanduiden, zoudt ge mij zeer verplichten', Virginie Loveling to Paul Fredericq, January 6, 1882, Van Elslander and Musschoot, 'Correspondentie van de Gezusters Loveling', p. 86.

53 Von Flotow, *Translation and Gender*, p. 76.

54 Hélène Swarth to the Erven Bohn, June 23, 1882, University Library Leiden, BOH C82. In 1884, she also asked the Belgian publisher De Seyn whether he was interested in a translation of Ouida's *Strathmore* (July 1884, AMVC, Album De Seyn, 25716/8bis), but this translation was apparently done by a Dutch friend of hers (July 3, 1884, AMVC Album De Seyn, 25730/5).

some effort from time to time into finding a book to translate, but have not succeeded'.[55] However, she would not accept just anything. Some years before she had refused to translate a drama by Betsy Perk that was in French verse because she did not consider its quality to be high enough.[56] It took a long time before she was commissioned to translate some works and even then she wrote to De Mont: 'Translating is repugnant to me, it takes too much time and it is very badly paid'.[57] Nevertheless, the translations she did do, especially after 1910, are generally regarded as high-quality work.[58] The authors she chose were both male and female and with whom she felt a definite connection.

Mina Sleeckx published her first translation as a separate volume (*Geoffroy en Garcinde*) and later published her translations and adaptations in *De Toekomst* (1857-1898), a pedagogical journal edited by her father and brother. As money was tight at the journal, almost none of its contributions were remunerated. Except for Logeman-van der Willigen, there were no professional women translators in Flanders who relied on their translations as their main source of income. Most were writers or teachers who were looking for extra money, although not all translations were remunerated and some were published mainly for content-based and ideological reasons, which will be elaborated in the next section.

Ideology and Canon Formation

In addition to the issue of remuneration, some translators also had a particular mission, revealing that 'translation has at times emerged as a strong form of expression for women – allowing them to enter the world

55 'Een woordje om u te vragen of gij ook een uitgever weet, die vertaalwerk niet te slecht betaalt. Ik deed nu en dan veel moeite om een boek te vertalen te krijgen, doch het mocht mij nooit gelukken', Hélène Swarth to Pol de Mont, September 14, 1887, *Hélène Swarth. Brieven aan Pol de Mont*, p. 122. On November 19, she wrote to De Mont that none of the recommended publishers had answered her plea, ibidem, p. 131. On July 15, she repeated that she had made a lot of effort to find source texts with no success, ibidem, p. 141.

56 Hélène Swarth to Pol de Mont, December 13, 1884, ibidem, p. 82.

57 'Vertalen staat mij tegen, neemt zeer veel tijd en wordt zeer slecht betaald', Hélène Swarth to Pol de Mont, July 10, 1891, ibidem, p. 222.

58 Jeroen Brouwers, *Hélène Swarth. Haar huwelijk met Frits Lapidoth, 1894-1910* (Amsterdam, 1985), p. 130.

of letters, to promote political causes and to engage in stimulating writing relationships'.[59] Here I will single out some content-based motives and some motives with regard to canon formation. With respect to the latter, in line with Rakefet Sela-Sheffy's argument in 'Canon Formation Revisited', two strategies can be discerned: consolidating and supporting an existing repertoire on the one hand, and prefiguring a future repertoire, on the other. Content-based motives can be further divided into two strands: politically motivated translations and didactic genres.

Some translators, such as Virginie Loveling, Swarth, Belpaire and Logeman-van der Willigen, acted as ambassadors for other styles or cultures, and introduced new repertoires, be it through their translations themselves or through their other critical activities. Virginie Loveling translated novels by the Low German writer Klaus Groth, whom she had personally met on his tour through Flanders.[60] She was introduced to the author and his work by Constant Jacob Hansen (1833-1910), a Groth fan who fancied her sister Rosalie, which supports Wilfert's view that coincidence plays an important role in the reception of an author.[61]

Groth's work was a revelation at the time, both in Germany and in Flanders, because it dealt with the common themes of patriotism, nature, domestic happiness or the beloved mother tongue in an innovative and realistic fashion. His style was concise, analytic and less pompous, while his psychological insight and striking detail were also praised, in contrast with the so-called 'perverted' style of the French novels and the more didactic literature of earlier authors such as Conscience and Ledeganck.[62] In her 1881 critical article in *l'Athenaeum belge*, Virginie Loveling praised Groth's moderate and precise language and psychological insight and thus prefigured a future canon. By translating Groth, an author writing in the peripheral language of Low German, she took part in a larger movement supported by other authors such as Guido Gezelle (1830-1899), Jan van Droogenbroeck (1835-1902) and De Mont, who all praised this author for his strong realism and defended his sound and healthy style against French literary influences.

59 Sherry Simon, *Gender in Translation. Cultural Identity and the Politics of Transmission* (London/New York, 1996), p. 39.

60 The Loveling sisters met Klaus Groth in August 1861, when he travelled through Belgium. Simons, *Vlaamse en Nederduitse literatuur in de 19de eeuw*, p. 334.

61 Wilfert, 'Cosmopolis et l'homme invisible', p. 37.

62 Simons, *Vlaamse en Nederduitse literatuur in de 19de eeuw*, pp. 338-343.

Logeman-van der Willigen functioned as a genuine ambassador for modern Danish, Swedish and Norwegian authors, introducing and commenting upon recently published work in numerous critical articles in journals such as *Scandia* (1904), *Scandinavia-Nederland* (1905-1906) – of which she was also an editor –, *De Vlaamsche Gids* (1905-1914)[63] and *De Week* (1909-1912).[64] She knew many authors personally, which led to an almost inexhaustible supply of new works and an enormous amount of enthusiasm in persuading publishers and editors to distribute or publish her translations. She was one of the rare women translators who actively took the initiative to import specific authors and works.[65]

To Max Rooses, the editor of *De Vlaamsche Gids*, she wrote: 'Herman Bang has offered me his *Personal Memories of Hendrik Ibsen* which is now available in Denmark. Could that be of interest for your review? If so, I'll translate it immediately so that you can publish it at once, otherwise it will be too late to be of any use. I beg you for a quick reply, if not, I'll offer them elsewhere'.[66] As well as using the social capital these authors passed on, she also tried to consolidate authors and prefigure a new literary generation. Additionally, it was also her view that smaller countries had to support each other in their struggle against the political and cultural ascendancy of larger nations such as France, Germany and Russia.[67]

Other writers, such as Van Ackere-Doolaeghe, Belpaire, Van Daelen and Germonprez were led by religious or politically inspired motives. Belpaire was fond of the Catholic writer Jørgensen and wanted to spread his word in Flanders. Van Ackere-Doolaeghe and Germonprez had a nationalist agenda with their publications, aiming at a defence of the Flemish culture and language. Van Ackere-Doolaeghe used her symbolic capital to defend the former liberal Minister of State, Rogier, against claims that he disliked

63 Besides the articles published in 1908, they were published in 1906, 1909 and 1910.

64 They appeared in *De Week* in 1910 and 1911.

65 Wilfert, 'Cosmopolis et l'homme invisible', p. 37, states that most translators who take the initiative themselves, are 'les traducteurs les plus artistes et les plus 'fidèles' à un auteur'. This does not hold true in the case of Logeman-van der Willigen.

66 '*Herman Bang* biedt me zijn "Persoonlijke Herinneringen over Hendrik Ibsen" aan, die heden in Denem. verschijnen. Zou dit niet iets zijn voor Uw blad? Ik vertaal ze dan dadelijk zodat U 't direct kunt plaatsen, anders is 't mosterd na de maaltijd! Verzoeke spoedig antwoord – daar ik ze anders elders geef', Dina Logeman-van der Willigen to Max Rooses, June 22, 1906, AMVC L 706/B2, no. 166169/2442.

67 Broomans, 'Vertalingen waar haast bij is', p. 59.

the use of the Dutch language in Flanders. In translating a French poem into Dutch, Van Ackere-Doolaeghe wanted to honour his literary talent and his often neglected support of Dutch literature. Her other translation of a poem by Longfellow was not politically inspired, but probably consolidated an existing repertoire. The sad and melancholy tone probably determined her choice in this case.

Fanny Delvaux, who was not well known when she published two translated poems by Heinrich Heine and John Henry Mackay, mainly used her translations to give voice to their and her anarchist beliefs. Heine's poem cursed God, king and country for not relieving the burden of the poor, and Mackay's poem defended the tenets of anarchism.

Some writers did not mention the authors of the translated works. Their motives were clearly content-based and they either undertook the task for pleasure or didactic purposes. Fanny Lava considered translating to be very enjoyable and particularly instructive, not so much because of the knowledge displayed in the work itself, but because it taught her how to write and meant she entered the world of letters.[68] She wrote to her son that she would be very pleased if he could find as much pleasure in translating as she had.[69] In a letter to Professor Thiery, a colleague of her husband, she wrote that she really loved Gogol's works. She thought that *Dead Souls* was perplexing for a Western reader but typically old-Russian, and regretted the low quality of most German translations.[70]

Like most of Paula and Mina Sleeckx's translations and Mathilda van Engelen's work, some of Lava's translated stories had a hidden message which became clear in the end. The translated folktales mainly dealt with the burden of life and the destiny and luck of the poor, who realise that property is not the most important aspect of life. The pedagogical value of the fairy tales was probably the reason why she translated and published them. Except for Victor Blüthgen and Hans Christian Andersen, none of the original authors were mentioned. The stories dealt with distant places but the motifs and characters were quite familiar: efforts are rewarded, the

68 Fanny MacLeod-Maertens to Andries MacLeod, May 30, 1917, University Library Uppsala.

69 Fanny MacLeod-Maertens to Andries MacLeod, June 6, 1917, University Library Uppsala.

70 Fanny MacLeod-Maertens to Michel Thiery, December 3, 1919, AMVC D128/B3, no. 177317/441.

burden of life is heavy, curiosity is punished and everything ends happily when one is modest, generous and helpful. These translations accorded with the didactic goals of many Flemish reviews and did not have any aspiration to influence the literary field of their time. They consolidated an existing repertoire without defending the canonisation of particular authors.

Symbolic Capital?

Making oneself known or entering the field does not seem to be a major motive behind translating. Both Virginie Loveling and Fanny Lava considered it good practice, but the former had already been publishing for a couple of years and the latter never had a literary career. Nevertheless, translating Groth's novels might have influenced Loveling's switch from poetry to prose.[71] Both Germonprez and Swarth primarily considered translating to be an activity that did not contribute to their literary careers. However, Loveling not only introduced Groth's work by translating it, her choice also suggests that she had common literary grounds with him and other realist European writers, which could have influenced future views on her own literary production. Groth's work showed the same choice of themes and style as the strategic options that seemed available to Loveling. She thus gained some symbolic capital that she, however, would lose again when a new literary generation appeared.

Apparently, none of the other women writers consciously opted for translating as a means to enhance their prestige. None of them explicitly expressed a desire to revive the canonised forms of expression. Although they did open up the local culture and enriched the language and domestic forms of expression, none took a radical stance in setting a new trend, thus refusing the most prestigious option in cultural transmission singled out by Rakefet Sela-Sheffy.[72] In contrast to France, where we can discern two contending groups in the mid-nineteenth century, the Symbolists and the Academics, who were competing for legitimacy and establishing particular repertoires in an autonomous field, there were no such clearly opposed groups in the not yet autonomous literary field in Flanders. For the greater part of the nineteenth century, Flemish writers were still bound

71 Simons, *Vlaamse en Nederduitse literatuur in de 19de eeuw*, p. 347.

72 Rakefet Sela-Sheffy, 'How to Be a (Recognized) Translator. Rethinking Habitus, Norms, and the Field of Translation', *Target* 17 (2005), p. 8.

by political ties and wrote partly to meet the needs of the public. As we have seen above, there was an opposition between nationalist, patriotic and pedagogical translators such as Van Ackere-Doolaeghe or Germonprez and translators such as Loveling and Logeman-van der Willigen, who were interested in more recent literature. However, the struggle to occupy certain positions in a stratified space with particular gains and losses was not fully present.

Virginie Loveling, ca. 1920, from Collection AMVC-Letterenhuis, Antwerp.

Following Sela-Sheffy's theoretical outline, we can conclude that the group of female translators in Flanders consisted of a rather invisible, semi-professional group whose translation work was often a side-project.[73] They were mostly individuals who did not benefit from some kind of group

73 Ibidem, p. 9.

affiliation and who were generally not well known for their translation activities. Antagonism, heresy or liberation from the established repertoire are not explicitly apparent as a primary motivation. The opposition between gatekeepers or cultural custodians, on the one hand, and trendsetters or cultural importers, on the other, is therefore not clearly marked. Consequently, there is also no clear distinction between a restricted elite of well-known translators and a wide circle of underprivileged anonymous agents – to use Sela-Sheffy's terminology.[74] Implicit status contests and a hidden struggle for symbolic capital were gradually becoming visible in the Flemish literary field, but did not yet infect translation as a socially organised activity.

Coda

In addition to these micro-stories and particular motives, and of course the available educational resources, one also has to bear in mind the larger picture. During the nineteenth century, Flanders was a highly Gallicised area in which the intellectual elite spoke and read French.[75] The middle and lower classes, on the other hand, opted for Dutch and were not always able to spend money on highbrow literature. Making money by publishing original or translated literature in Dutch was therefore no sinecure at all. There was little public interest in Dutch translations – which made Virginie Loveling and Swarth consider translating into French – and there was also an underdeveloped publishing trade, in which booksellers and printers still filled the roles of editors.

Logeman-van der Willigen and Swarth published the largest part of their oeuvre in the Netherlands, despite competition from other translators being greater. Only by choosing small languages (a proficiency evidently not acquired at school) or combining translation work with another profession were they able to earn a decent living. Contributions to cultural and literary magazines were not always remunerated, and translations mostly yielded an additional profit only. Both Virginie Loveling and Swarth complained of the difficulties in finding interested editors or publishers who wanted to pay for their translated work.

Reading the correspondence of these writers, it seems that the translations of literary works in Flanders between 1870 and 1914 were a

74 Ibidem, p. 21.

75 Klinkenberg, 'De Franse literatuur in Vlaanderen', p. 517.

matter of coincidence, linguistic proficiency and chance contacts made with particular editors and authors. It was not a practice chosen to enhance one's own prestige or make oneself known as a budding writer in the field. Nevertheless, ideological motives with regard to politics or education, and motives concerning canon formation, whether this meant importing new authors or consolidating an existing repertoire, played a modest but real part.

Appendix

Belpaire, M.-E., *Klokke Roeland* (Bussum, 1916).

Belpaire, M.-E., *Sinnoeve Solbakken* (Maldeghem, 1902).

Belpaire, M.-E., *De jongste dag* (Antwerp, 1900).

Belpaire, M.-E., *Levensleugen en levenswaarheid* (Ghent, 1900).

Germonprez, A., 'Drumsheugh's Liefdesgeschiedenis [Ian Maclaren]', *Dietsche Warande en Belfort* 2 (1901), pp. 455-477, 584-596.

Hiel, L., 'Wat waren die rozen toch frisch en schoon (naar een prozastukje van Tourguenef)', *Vlaamsch & Vrij* 3 (1895), p. 633.

Hiel, L., '*Jehova* van Carmen Sylva. Vrij naar het Duitsch', *Vlaamsch & Vrij* 2 (1894), pp. 675, 712, 751.

Hiel, L., 'Grieksch Liefdeverhaal. Uit de Grieksche Volksverhalen', *Vlaamsch & Vrij* 1 (1893), p. 7.

Kropotin, P., *Idealen en werkelijkheid in de Russische literatuur, uit het Engelsch vert. door Fanny Mac Leod-Maertens* (Amsterdam, 1907).

Kropotin, P., *Wederkeerig dienstbetoon, een factor der evolutie; voorafgegaan door Strijd voor het bestaan en wederkeerig dienstbetoon, met toestemming van den schrijver uit het Engels vertaald door Fanny Mac Leod-Maertens* (Amsterdam, 1904).

Logeman-van der Willigen, D., *De vluchtelingen* [Johannes Linnankoski] (Antwerp, 1914).

Logeman-van der Willigen, D., 'Persoonlijke herinneringen aan Henrik Ibsen van Herman Bang', *De Vlaamsche Gids* 2 (1906), pp. 475-488.

Logeman-van der Willigen, D., *De paradijsvogel* [Otto Rung] (Antwerp, s.d).

Loveling, R., 'Trina', *Het Letterkundig Zondagsblad* 7 (1864), pp. 11-24.

Loveling, V., 'Witen Slachters. Nog een vertelling uit mijn jongheidsparadijs. Naar het Platduitsch van Klaus Groth', *Nederlandsch Museum* 9 (1882), pp. 316-348.

Loveling, V., 'Drei plattdeutsche Erzählungen zum Theil Erlebtes und Erinnerungen von 1848 aus Schleswig-Holstein, von Klaus Groth', *Athenaeum belge* 5 (1881), pp. 51-52.

Loveling, V., 'Een Holsteinsche jongen. Naar het Platduitsch van Klaus Groth [a revised version of *Detelf*]', *Nederlandsch Museum* 7 (1880), pp. 174-268.

Loveling, V., 'Antoon (van Quickborn). Naar het Platduitsch van Klaus Groth [translation of *De Waterbörs*]', *Het Nederduitsch Tijdschrift* 4 (1866 I), pp. 47-85.

Loveling, V., 'Detel. Naar het Platduitsch van Klaus Groth [translation of Detelf]', *Het Nederduitsch Tijdschrift* 4 (1866 II), pp. 27-64.

MacLeod-Maertens, F., 'Mengeling. Een handvol aarde (Oostersche vertelling)', *Het Vaderland* 11 mei 1894.

MacLeod-Maertens, F., 'Mengeling. De last (translated from the Russian journal *Niwa*)', *Het Vaderland* 8 juni 1894.

MacLeod-Maertens, F., 'Vier Dagen. Uit het Russisch vertaald', *Gazette van Ghent* (1894), pp. 3-4.

Programmes de l'enseignement à donner dans les écoles normales et les sections normales primaires de l'état (Ghent, 1892).

Rijckaerts, E., *Jeronimo: verzamelde novellen door Anna Germonprez; met voorrede en levensschets van de schrijfster* (Antwerp, 1950).

Sleeckx, M., 'Twee Slavische sprookjes. I. De taal der dieren; II. Het wijze vonnis', *De Toekomst* 26 (1882), pp. 455-467.

Sleeckx, M., 'De Pochhans [Victor Blüthgen]', *De Toekomst* 25 (1881), pp. 306-312.

Sleeckx, M., 'Paascheieren', *De Toekomst* 23 (1879), pp. 311-315.

Sleeckx, M., 'De Padde. Een sprookje uit Esthland', *De Toekomst* 22 (1878), pp. 119-124.

Sleeckx, M., 'Marten. Een Hoogduitsch sprookje', *De Toekomst* 21 (1877), pp. 97-101.

Sleeckx, M., *Geoffroy en Garcinde* [Paul Heyse] ('s Gravenhage, 1873).

Sleeckx, M., *De Twaalf Apostelen* [Eugenie Marlitt] (Antwerp, s.d.).

Sleeckx, M., *Het geheim van den ouden kaemer* [Emile Mario Vacano] (Antwerp, s.d.).

Sleeckx, P., 'Dragen en verdragen (naar Katharina Koch)', *De Toekomst* 20 (1876), p. 206.

Stinissen, E., 'Iets over Pestalozzi (vrij naar eenen reisbrief van Emil Schattke)', *De Toekomst* 41 (1895-1896), pp. 529-535.

Swarth, H., *Hélène Swarth. Brieven aan Pol de Mont* (Ghent, 1964).

Swarth, H., *Haar lente* [Rachilde] (Amsterdam, 1913).

Swarth, H., *De nachten, metrisch overgezet en ingeleid door Hélène Swarth* [Alfred de Musset] (Amsterdam, 1912).

Swarth, H., 'Gedichten in proza [Oscar Wilde]', *Europa. Maandschrift voor Nederlandsche en vreemde letteren* (1910) [no copies of this issue have survived].

Swarth, H., *Roemeensche volksliederen en balladen* [Hélène Vacaresco] (Amsterdam, 1909).

Swarth, H., 'Een Doode: Théodore Aubanel, door Charles Fuster', *Nederlandsche Dicht- en Kunsthalle* 11 (1888), pp. 339-342.

Swarth, H., 'Lied van A. von Platen. Sonnet XLIV van A. von Platen', *Nederlandsche Dicht- en Kunsthalle* 8 (1886), pp. 525-526.

Swarth, H., *La paix durable* [Johannes Allarda] (Bussum, s.d.).

Swarth, H., *Portugeesche sonnetten* [Elizabeth Barrett Browning] (Amsterdam, s.d.).

Van Ackere-Doolaeghe, M., 'Het open venster. Naar het Engelsch van Longfellow', *De Toekomst* 27 (1883), p. 253.

Van Ackere-Doolaeghe, M., 'De laatste zang van Lord Byron. In Griekenland', *Nederlandsche Dicht- en Kunsthalle* 5 (1882), pp. 161-162.

Van Ackere-Doolaeghe, M., 'De tehuiskomst. Naar "Le Retour à la maison" van M. Ch. Rogier, Minister van Staat', *De Vlaamsche Kunstbode* 2 (1872), pp. 112-117.

Van Daelen, S., 'Liedjes van Opstand. De Wevers (van Heinrich Heine)', *Ontwaking* 8 (1907), p. 270.

Van Daelen, S., 'Liedjes van Opstand. Anarchie (John Henry Mackay)', *Ontwaking* 8 (1907), p. 271.

Van Elslander, A. and Musschoot, A.M., 'Correspondentie van de Gezusters Loveling. Brieven van en aan Paul Fredericq II', *Mededelingen van het Cyriel Buysse Genootschap* 10 (1994), pp. 31-156.

Van Engelen, M., 'De Huisduiveltjes. Een sprookje uit Scandinavië', *De Toekomst* 23 (1879), pp. 16-20.

Gendering Cultural Transfer and Transmission History

« Petra Broomans and Marta Ronne »

Looking back on the research done within the project 'Peripheral Autonomy?', it is apparent that a specific group of translators was the subject of our research: women who were knocking on the door of 'translation canon heaven'. Within this context, the participants in the project rediscovered lost material and developed new insights into individual women translators who had completed many translations but were only acknowledged in single sentences in studies on reception history. An example in Grit's *Driewerf zalig Noorden* is Dina Logeman-van der Willigen (1864-1925) who, though a very active and productive translator, was mentioned only once alongside other women translators.[1] In addition, translators who we thought were no longer with us, such as Greta Baars-Jelgersma (1911), were 'found' and interviewed, ultimately providing all concerned with many new insights into the translation business.[2] It became clear that an important field had not yet been thoroughly investigated and that a lot of material was waiting to be discovered and made public.

Starting point

From Darwin to Weil. Women as Transmitters of Ideas (2009), the first volume of the Studies on Cultural Transfer and Transmission series, discussed the way that women translators and introducers of foreign

1 Diederik C. Grit, *Driewerf zalig Noorden. Over literaire betrekkingen tussen de Nederlanden en Scandinavië* (Maastricht, 1994), p. 119. See the article by Ester Jiresch, 'Marie-Elisabeth Belpaire and Dina Logeman-Van der Willigen. Two Cultural Transmitters in Flanders – in the Same Literary Field?', in: Petra Broomans and Marta Ronne, eds., *In the Vanguard of Cultural Transfer. Cultural Transmitters and Authors in Peripheral Literary Fields* (Groningen, 2010), pp. 33-54.

2 Janke Klok, 'Greta Baars-Jelgersma, Cora Sandel and the Dutch Literary Field, 1925-1950. Aspects of Cross-national Literary Transfer', in: Broomans and Ronne, *In the Vanguard*, pp. 55-88.

literature transmitted ideas to the Dutch-speaking region and to Scandinavia. The volume formed one of the starting points within the 'Peripheral Autonomy?' project for rethinking gender in the field of cultural transfer and transmission. In the introduction, a working definition of the cultural transmitter was formulated, a historical overview of the role of women in literary history and the translation trade was provided and previous research on the topic was discussed.[3] One of the conclusions was that '[a] transnational and comparative history of the role of women cultural transmitters has not yet been written'.[4]

The term cultural transmitter was chosen because translators take various roles and positions in different periods. A cultural transmitter 'basically works within a particular language and culture area' and 'takes on various roles (...): translator, reviewer, critic, journalist, literary historian, scholar, teacher, librarian, book seller, collector, literary agent, scout, publisher, editor of a journal, writer, travel writer or counsellor'.[5]

The various essays undertook studies of women in the book market and in the field of translations, travel and other forms of journalism, and literary critique in small language communities from the mid-1860s to the early 1950s. The focus was on the 'making of' a cultural transmitter in these different fields, investigating the transmitter's social background, her education, her ability to create networks and the ideas she mediated. Furthermore, the relationship between the centre and the periphery (in two senses: in terms of dominating versus small language areas, and men versus women in the literary field) was scrutinised. Various ways of transmitting ideas came to the fore: women transmitted ideas as correspondents and travellers (Camilla Collett),[6] as translators (Virginie Loveling, Margaretha Meyboom, Margit Abenius), as critics and journalists (Marie-Elisabeth Belpaire and other contributors to *Dietsche Warande en Belfort*, Laura Marholm, Margit Abenius) and as writers and debaters (Virginie Loveling, Laura Marholm, Margit Abenius).

3 Petra Broomans, 'Introduction: Women as Transmitters of Ideas', in: Petra Broomans, ed., *From Darwin to Weil. Women as Transmitters of Ideas* (Groningen, 2009), pp. 1-20.

4 Broomans, 'Introduction', p. 20.

5 Broomans, 'Introduction', p. 2.

6 See also Brian Dolan's study *Ladies of the Grand Tour. British Women in Pursuit of Enlightenment and Adventure in Eighteenth-Century Europe* (New York, 2001).

The theoretical framework in *From Darwin to Weil* covered various elements. One institutional aspect concentrated on Pierre Bourdieu's concept of the cultural field, including terms such as 'symbolic capital' and 'habitus', as well as feminist interpretations of Bourdieu such as those of Moi and Sniader Lanser.[7] Another institutional and societal approach involved research on networks of women using Boissevain's Social Network Analysis (SNA) and McFadden's study, which contributed a feminist turn in SNA.[8] It was found that the terms 'cultural *transfer*', defined as the one-way activity of translation from one language into another, and 'cultural *transmission*', a reciprocal situation in which cultural and literary information is shared,[9] could be elaborated on at other levels and related to private and professional spheres. The conditions or prerequisites for such events are also both personal and professional, including language skills, networks, cultural capital, social capital, economic means, aesthetic, ideological, political or economic motives, and last but not least, a very sharp pen or, as in the case of the Swede Margit Abenius (1899-1970), eloquence in mediating literature through radio broadcasting.[10] These capacities can be acted out and brought to bear in the private sphere and in different professional environments. This illustrates once again the flexibility and versatility of cultural transmitters. To take Abenius as an example once again, she not only mediated literature in the public sphere of broadcasting but also in a more private sphere, as the leader of a women's reading group whose meetings took place in an intimate atmosphere. This

7 Toril Moi, 'Appropriating Bourdieu. Feminist Theory and Pierre Bourdieu's Sociology of Culture', *New Literary History*, 4 (1991), pp. 1017-1049; Susan Sniader Lanser and Evelyn Torton Beck, '[Why] Are There No Great Women Critics? And What Difference Does It Make?', in: Julia A. Sherman and Evelyn Torton Beck, eds., *The Prism of Sex. Essays on the Sociology of Knowledge* (Madison, 1979), pp. 79-91; Jeja-Pekka Roos and Anna Rotkirch, 'Fält i skuggan av fält; sensocialismens dubbelliv', in: Donald Broady, ed., *Kulturens fält. En antologi* (Gothenburg, 1998), pp. 453-466; Lisa Adkins and Beverley Skeggs, *Feminism After Bourdieu* (Oxford, 2004).

8 Jeremy Boissevain, *Friends of Friends: Networks, Manipulators and Coalitions* (Oxford, 1974); Margaret H. McFadden, *Golden Cables of Sympathy. The Transatlantic Sources of Nineteenth Century Feminism* (Lexington, 1999).

9 Petra Broomans, 'Preface', in: Broomans, *From Darwin to Weil*, p. VII.

10 Marta Ronne, '"There is Always an Invisible Reader..." The Swedish Critic Margit Abenius and the Making of a Female Cultural Transmitter', in: Broomans and Ronne, *In the Vanguard*, pp. 106-113.

shows that in different circumstances Abenius had to act in different ways and use different skills.[11]

Margit Abenius (1899-1970). From Uppsala University Library.

A useful instrument within the 'Peripheral Autonomy?' project was the internet forum designed after the first workshop in Ghent 2006. Several articles dealing with theoretical questions within the field of cultural transfer and transmission were published on this forum. The volume *From*

11 Margit Abenius commented on this in her *Memoarer från det inre* (Stockholm, 1963). Her different roles are currently being studied by Marta Ronne, see 'Läsandets ambassadör', to be published in spring 2013.

Darwin to Weil and the articles on the forum functioned as the point of departure for the next three volumes: *In the Vanguard of Cultural Transfer. Cultural Transmitters and Authors in Peripheral Literary Fields* (2010), *The Invasion of Books in Peripheral Literary Fields. Transmitting Preferences and Images in Media, Networks and Translation* (2011) and this volume, *Rethinking Cultural Transfer and Transmission. Reflections and New Perspectives* (2012).

In the Vanguard

In the Vanguard of Cultural Transfer primarily focused on individual cultural transmitters in small language communities (generally women), mediating both between countries (Scandinavia to the Netherlands) and between language minorities (Nynorsk in Norway, Swedish-Finnish in Finland), from the late nineteenth century until 1950. Attention was paid to both highbrow and other channels of transmission. The cultural transmitters involved showed a versatility that supports the idea of the cultural transmitter as having various roles. The transmission of literature, culture and ideas was carried out by writers and cultural mediators (Arne and Hulda Garborg), translators and critics (Marie-Elisabeth Belpaire, Dina Logeman-van der Willigen, Greta Baars-Jelgersma, Hagar Olsson and Margit Abenius), and by critics and writers promoting, for example, *flâneur* literature and translations from Finnish to Swedish (such as those by Hagar Olsson). The theoretical tools were taken from the articles published on the forum: Petra Broomans' model of five stages of transmission, Johan Heilbron's and Gisèle Sapiro's reflections on social, political and economic aspects of translation and culture transfer, Reine Meylaerts' proposals on Polysystem Theory (PST) and Descriptive Translation Studies (DTS) and Joep Leerssen's paper on history and the method of imagology in literary studies.[12] The theoretical frameworks applied in *From Darwin to Weil* were also used in the current volume. They also include gender theory, feminist readings of Bourdieu and research on networks.

12 See http://www.soctat.org.

Hagar Olsson, probably 1920s.

Invasion

The Invasion of Books in Peripheral Literary Fields (2011) concentrated on the professionalisation and globalisation of the field of cultural transfer and transmission in the period between 1950 and the present day. It investigated the function and appreciation of the literature transmitted in the media, such as women's magazines, as well as the role of cultural transmitters, examining their networks and asking why in some cases they disappeared from the field of cultural transfer and transmission history (for example, Annie Posthumus). The connection between changing national identities and the varying definitions of national and minority literatures was also discussed, with an exile writer such as Zenta Mauriņa, a German-speaking Latvian writer who attempted to establish herself as a writer and critic in Sweden, being a special case. As an exile writer, intellectual and a translator, she worked with 'cultural transmission from within'.

Annie Posthumus (1881-1964) in 1954, at the age of 73 still active as a cultural transmitter. Photo courtesy of B.J. Kruimel, family archive.

Against the backdrop of globalisation, various centres and peripheries changed positions. However, *The Invasion of Books* also found that in addition to institutions, individual actors such as cultural transmitters are still playing essential roles in cultural transfer, despite the growing significance of the commercial environment. In this volume it becomes clear that ideas, images and preferences for foreign literatures were expressed through the media (newspapers, magazines, literary journals) and networks of authors and critics. Ethnic minority literatures, for example a minority language such as Nynorsk, as well as the images of women that were conveyed, were discussed and transmitted in the media. The means of transmission are shown to have become more complex. In this volume, agents such as newspapers and magazines were investigated more than individual mediators, with their representation of ethnic minority literatures and languages being the focus. The individual women cultural transmitters who are discussed, worked within and outside academia, as critics, translators, authors and counsellors and took on various other roles. Despite being so active in the various phases of the cultural transfer process, they nevertheless vanished from cultural transfer and transmission history.

Various feminist scholars such as Louise von Flotow and Susanne Stark have reflected on the reasons why women translators disappeared from reception and literary history. Did 'women translators (...) [consider] themselves as merely useful tools for the reproduction of the admired text of a beloved author, or as active mediators who made their own choices'?[13] In other words, did they take part because of their attitude to the original text or were they, like women writers, regarded as 'exceptions', to be discussed in separate 'gynaecea' surveys and excluded from regular literary histories? We will discuss this question in the last part of this essay.

As in the previous volumes, the Bourdieuian perspective was used, as described in the article by Heilbron and Sapiro available on the internet forum, and the concept of minor literature from Deleuze and Guattari was also applied. One of the conclusions was that against the backdrop of globalisation, commercialisation and the need for transnational canons, the importance and the various roles of individuals and groups of cultural transmitters are still underestimated today.

Rethinking

With respect to gender, the current volume, *Rethinking Cultural Transfer and Transmission*, continues to explore previous threads, such as women cultural transmitters in Flanders between 1870 and 1914 and the role of networks. One new perspective that is introduced here in the research proposal by Karina Smits concerns the meaning of cultural transfer for lesbian magazines. Another contribution scrutinised the 'citational universe' of Swedish literary scholarship with respect to gender and found that English departments favour feminist and female-authored criticism. Other new research lines concern reflections on how to write translation

13 See Broomans, 'Introduction', p. 12; Louise von Flotow, *Translation and Gender. Translating in the 'Era of Feminism'* (Manchester/Ottowa, 1997); Susanne Stark, *'Behind inverted commas'. Translation and Aglo-German Cultural Relations in the Nineteenth Century* (Clevedon, 1999).

history, the importance of storytelling as a survival strategy for the Sami minority, and a research proposal concerning migrant literature (for a general overview of the volume see the introduction).

In summary, throughout the project the work of Bourdieu in particular, or an elaborated Bourdieuian framework, was used, with a 'gendered' Bourdieuian framework addressing gender issues. Network analysis and the analysis of social factors behind literature production was also applied. The creation of unequal conditions between women and men in the literary field was made visible, while the analysis of a gendered book market, of gendered fields of cultural production, and a discussion of the relationship between small and large language areas and large and small literatures were continuous threads throughout the project. Attention was paid to new groups entering the field, such as ethnic minorities and lesbian agents in the literary field.

Towards a polyvoiced canon

Should we consider 'Women Cultural Transmitters' versus 'Men Cultural Transmitters', or perhaps concentrate on 'Cultural Transmitters' as such? How can we make unequal conditions *visible* without *essentialising* them in modern literary gender research? Could this dilemma point to a strategic new approach to literary history to solve the old dilemma?

Before making some suggestions for a more balanced cultural transfer and transmission history, we will discuss what has been done in the field of literary history. The keyword here is also *rethinking*. According to Hutcheon and Valdés, '[r]ethinking is not only thinking again; it is thinking anew'.[14] It means a dynamic view of literary history and a change of paradigm for literary research. They define literary history as a set of multiple histories of literary production and reception, which are parts of social, economic and political history, where gender, class and ethnicity are also important factors.[15] The Swedish scholar Lisbeth Stenberg adapted the ideas of Hutcheon and Valdés in her study of literary debates, arguing that '[a]n open literary history is connected to other research disciplines

14 Linda Hutcheon and Mario J. Valdés, *Rethinking Literary History. A Dialogue on Theory* (Oxford, 2002), p. X.

15 Ibidem. See also the entire preface, 'Theorizing Literary History in Dialogue', pp. IX-XIII.

and it describes both continuity and change. It is clearly situated and it explores how images, tropes and representations of the world are produced within the cultural imaginary'.[16]

In her analyses of power relationships in literature production and in research on literary history, literature is seen as a way of constructing identities, and discussions of the concept of the literary canon and the methods of writing literary history are also presented. Stenberg makes an attempt to present a more 'effective' and 'open' view of literary production in Sweden around 1900, '[t]raditional literary history tends to give a static picture of literary production, a picture that should rather be replaced by dynamic analysis of culture imaginaries'.[17]

Valdés himself has defined 'effective' literary history as follows:

> The tradition of literary history in the various literary histories, especially in western Europe and the Americas designates a formal style of interconnectedness that assures the continuity of the reception of the literary past. (...) In this respect it designates the reciprocity between us and the literary past. But what the tradition leaves out - the material contextualization of literature - makes this reciprocity a self-serving appropriation of the past. Full reciprocity is between a contextualized literary past and the awareness of our being affected by the literary past. This is what I have been calling effective literary history.[18]

Hutcheon and Valdés, as well as Stenberg, can be regarded as responding to scepticism in the field of literary historiography and in the analyses of

16 'En öppen litteraturhistoria anknyter till andra vetenskapliga grenar och beskriver både kontinuitet och förändring. Den är tydligt situerad och undersöker litterär kultur vad gäller produktion, spridning och reception av bilder, troper och framställningar av världen', Lisbeth Stenberg, *I kärlekens namn. Om människosynen, den nya kvinnan och framtidens samhälle i fem litteraturdebatter 1881-1909* (Stockholm, 2009), pp. 351-352.

17 '[D]en traditionella historieskrivningen [tenderar] att ge en statisk bild av gångna tiders litteraturproduktion, en bild som i stället bör ersättas med dynamiska analyser av lika dynamiska litterära kulturer', Stenberg, *I kärlekens namn*, p. 9.

18 Mario J. Valdés, 'Rethinking the History of Literary History', in: Hutcheon and Valdés, *Rethinking Literary History*, pp. 64-65.

the literary historiographical discourse in the 1980s and 1990s.[19] In the 2000s, debates about the notion of a 'canon' refocused on the possibility of a national canon and thus required a rethinking of literary history, as attempted by Hutcheon and Valdés, amongst others.

While Perkins, for example, discussed the possibility/impossibility of writing a national or other totalising form of literary history, feminist scholars brought new perspectives and/or wrote women's literary histories. Joanna Russ offers a succinct description of the perspective that was being explored: 'a multitude of centres of value, each with its own periphery, some closer to each other, some further apart'.[20] This opened up the possibility of a polyvoiced canon.

These perspectives can be a point of departure for a gendered cultural transfer and transmission history and are also of importance to cultural transfer and transmission studies in general. When pursuing an open literary history, existing histories must be rewritten and opened up to excluded groups, with no exceptions. To date, a women's cultural field remains in the shadows.[21] To rewrite literary history with the aim of including women, ethnic and minority groups, a critical rereading of the sources (newspaper debates, archives, etc.) is needed, while the collection and digitalisation of the material and the design of databases is of fundamental importance. Such work was already proposed by Margaret J.M. Ezell in 1993. Since then projects such as www.womenwriters.nl and the database created by Els Biesemans have been undertaken and are

19 See for example David Perkins, *Is Literary History Possible?* (Baltimore/London, 1992); Anna Williams, *Stjärnor utan stjärnbilder. Kvinnor och kanon i litteraturhistoriska översiktsverk under 1900-talet* (Uppsala, 1997); Petra Broomans, *Detta är jag. Stina Aronsons litteraturhistoriska öde* (Stockholm, 2001), with a discourse analysis (according to an adapted Hayden White analysis model) of the literary historiographical discourses in Nordic literary histories concerning women writers.

20 Joanna Russ, 'Anomalousness' and 'Aesthetics', in: Robyn R. Warhol and Diane Price Herndel, eds., *Feminisms. An Anthology of Literary Theory and Criticism* (New Brunswick/New Jersey, 1991), p. 210.

21 See Roos and Rotkirch, 'Fält i skuggan av fält', pp. 453-466.

fine examples of the collection and digitalisation of material.[22] Network analysis will also need to map the different fields in which women writers and women cultural transmitters were operating, and whether or not these fields are regarded as dominant (centre) or shadow fields (periphery).

The same mechanisms of exclusion are present in the field of cultural transfer and transmission. Cultural transmitters have been included or excluded from the canon for different reasons. Male authors in the nineteenth century who were also active as translators are included, while women translators are often regarded as 'assistants' who need not be included in reception and/or literary history. Are there any imperative criteria for the canonisation of a cultural transmitter? What qualities and skills do they need? What strategies or rules are required to gain capital in the literary field in order to enter literary and cultural transfer history? Could it be that visibility in the phases of the cultural transfer process, connection with important authors and/or mainstreams, awards, networks and professionalisation support canonisation? The role of cultural transmitters – and one should add, more specifically, women cultural transmitters – remains undervalued in literary history, cultural transfer studies, cultural studies and translation studies. Against the backdrop of new fields such as transnational literary histories and cultural transfer histories, a rethinking of cultural transfer and transmission history is needed. An ongoing dialogue between the fields of literary critique and that of cultural transfer and transmission that is not only concerned with the role of language and literature but also the roles of religion, women, national and ethnic identities, minorities, etc., could be a possible arena and source for such a rethinking. Suitable strategies would include making transmitters and their contributions visible in a broader context (networks, debate about religion, political motives, etc.) and demonstrating that women transmitters did not see themselves as merely 'women transmitters' but as transmitters and producers of culture.[23] To achieve this, more archive work has to be done and the documentation

22 Margaret J.M. Ezell, *Writing Women's Literary History* (Baltimore, 1993); http://www.womenwriters.nl; Els Biesemans, Vertalers van Scandinavische literatuur naar het Nederlands tussen 1860 en 1940. Evolutie van de samenstelling van de groep van vertalers en hun ideologische, maatschappelijke en professionele voorkeuren, 2013 (doctoral dissertation, in print).

23 See for example Geraldine Reymenants, 'Catholicism as a Stepping Stone to Authorship. The Contribution of Women to the Flemish Catholic Periodical *Dietsche Warande en Belfort*', in: Broomans, *From Darwin to Weil*, pp. 121-137.

of their profession in letters or other ego/self-biographical documents studied. Is it possible to deduce from this material a 'professional ego' of the cultural transmitter concerned? A mapping of the various conditions, the environment, milieu, education and the personal lives of the cultural transmitters will provide an outline of the inequality of gender conditions. A more profound knowledge of the private and professional lives of women and male cultural transmitters, their self-fashioning and position in the phases of the cultural transfer and transmission process can ultimately lead us away from the gendered worlds of literary history, paving the way towards complex but exciting studies in a versatile field of cultural transfer and transmission studies.

Epilogue

Gendering cultural transfer and transmission history has to deal with mechanisms of inclusion and exclusion originating from outside the field as well as from within. As long as well-known scholars such as Peter Burke and Michel Espagne only include women briefly or not at all in such studies, gendering the field will remain programmatic and thus strategic and political.[24] At the same time, a certain awareness of the discourse that is used has now been acquired. Thus, a gendered cultural transfer and transmission history can be programmatic but need not succumb to the pitfall of romanticism. A tendency in women's literary histories is to present women authors as heroines: 'feminist literary historical politics are combined with a romantic genius plot á la Hayden White and a focus on originality á la Harold Bloom'.[25] In contrast to this, our own discourse must be continually reconsidered and reflected upon.

24 Peter Burke, *Lost (and Found) in Translation: A Cultural History of Translators and Translating in Early Modern Europe* (Wassenaar, 2005); Michel Espagne, 'Jenseits der Komparatistik. Zur Methode der Erforschung von Kulturtransfers', in: Ulrich Mölk, ed., *Europäische Kulturzeitschriften um 1900 als Medien transnationaler und transdisziplinärer Wahrnehmung* (Abhandlungen der Akademie der Wissenschaften zu Göttingen, Philologisch-Historische Klasse, Dritte Folge, Bd. 273) (Göttingen, 2006), pp. 13-32.

25 Petra Broomans, 'In the name of God and the Father. Scandinavian women's literary history from a meta-literary historical point of view', in: Suzan van Dijk, Lia van Gemert and Sheila Ottway, eds., *Writing the History of Women's Writing. Towards an international approach* (Amsterdam, 2001), p. 133.

Dina Logeman-van der Willigen, March 1923. University Library Ghent.

However, the problem of genius remains. Does it lie with the splendid translator or the beloved author? And what about originality? Can it be found in the outstanding translation or only the original text? Should we regard these two opposites as peripheries/centres without borders? We suggest an active, effective, dynamic and polyvoiced cultural transfer and transmission history that is full of dynamic women, rather than a static cultural transfer and transmission history that is exclusive and monotoned.

Die Freundin and Other Relationships

A Proposal for a Comparative Study of the Role of Lesbian Magazines within the Process of Cultural Transfer and Transmission

« Karina Smits »

Introduction

Different minorities have been discussed in the Studies on Cultural Transfer and Transmission series. In a society in which heterosexuality is to a large extent the norm it would also be interesting to take a closer look at homosexuality within the field of cultural transfer and transmission. In this article, in which I will describe a proposal for a study on this subject, I will focus on lesbian magazines and their role within this process. One can imagine the importance of magazines for lesbian women as a group. This kind of activism affirms lesbian visibility and as such makes it possible for women to find others with similar desires and realise they are not alone.[1]

According to Remieg Aerts, magazines are special historical sources because they provide information about the state of affairs concerning knowledge, political and social views, the reception of new ideas or theories and international movements in a certain period. For Aerts, magazines, in comparison with a book or an author for example, are representative of a group during a particular period of time. At the same time, of course, one should consider that this representativeness is relative because every magazine represents only one aspect of one part of society.[2]

When we take a look at lesbian magazines published in various countries we find great differences. While gay magazines originated relatively early on, the role of women in these magazines and their relevance to women varied between countries. In the Dutch magazine *Vriendschap* (1949-1964), lesbian women played a marginal role until the 1960s, although the magazine was not solely directed at homosexual men. The first periodical

1 Leila Rupp, *Sapphistries. A Global History of Love between Women* (New York/London, 2009), p. 200.

2 Remieg Aerts, 'Het tijdschrift als culturele factor en als historische bron', *Groniek* 135 (1996), pp. 178-180.

that was directed specifically at homosexual women was *Amarant* (*Baal* until 1978), which was founded in 1971 and still exists.[3] In contrast, in the United States the first lesbian rights organisation, the Daughters of Bilitis (1955), published their own magazine *The Ladder* between 1956 and 1972. Moreover, in Germany, there were a couple of lesbian magazines in circulation even before the Second World War. *Die Freundin*, for example, was published between 1924 and 1933 and *Frauenliebe* between 1926 and 1930, then under the name *Garçonne* until 1932.[4]

Preliminary work

Before turning to the content of the study it is necessary to define a couple of terms as well as the research material. Concerning the description of cultural transfer and transmission, I restrict myself at this point to Petra Broomans' distinction between both terms. She regards cultural *transfer* as a one-way activity in which a text is translated from one language into another, while cultural *transmission* is reciprocal, with cultural and literary information being shared.[5] The main questions of this proposal reflect these definitions: In what way do lesbian magazines and their contents influence each other? How do they share information and ideas?

It is also important to determine what is meant by 'lesbian magazine'. A magazine is a periodical that comes out regularly, at least more than once a year but not on a daily basis. It is meant to offer information about a certain subject or to a certain audience.[6] Dutch writer Gerrit Komrij has summarised 'gay literature' as literature which has been written by, for or

3 Evert van der Veen, 'De Nederlandse homo-pers: historie, omvang en bereik', in: Edwin Bakker and Judith Schuyf, eds., *Homoseksualiteit en de media. Verslag van een studiedag georganiseerd door Homo RTV Urania en Homostudies Utrecht* (Utrecht, 1985), pp. 61-64, 70, 86; *Amarant* is the newsletter of 'Stichting Groep 7152', a national organisation directed at lesbian and bisexual women.

4 During the 1920s the term 'Garçonne-type' appeared, which applied to 'new' or 'emancipated' women who adopted a masculine style of dress and behaviour. The magazine *Garçonne* was aimed at a lesbian and male heterosexual transvestite audience. Rupp, *Sapphistries*, pp. 193-196.

5 Petra Broomans, 'Preface', in: Petra Broomans, ed., *From Darwin to Weil. Women as Transmitters of Ideas* (Groningen, 2009), p. VII.

6 Anne Dijkman, *Opzij & aan de kant met haar. De constructie van norm en afwijking in Opzij tussen 1972 en 2002* (Nijmegen, 2008), p. 25.

Cover of the German lesbian magazine Die Freundin, May 1928.
Source: http://www.cabaret-berlin.com/?p=659.

about gays, where at least two of these conditions are met.[7] One could also apply these conditions to a definition of lesbian magazines. Some problems are encountered, however, when looking at different magazines, as there are magazines that are considered to be feminist which also address lesbian issues, magazines that focus on bisexual women as well, and magazines for

7 http://www.homogeschiedenis.nl/thema/?onm3_catId=26, accessed August 1, 2012.

homosexual men and lesbian women. Can they all be included? As a result of the diversity, it might be necessary to also consider the definition of 'lesbian' more closely. Different words concerning homosexuality have had different meanings in different cultures and periods of time. However, in this proposal I will not examine this any further.

In addition to the definition of 'lesbian magazine', the research material must also be clearly defined. I have chosen 1924 as the starting point because *Die Freundin* was the first lesbian magazine ever published, while 2000 is the final point, meaning the research period covers well over 75years. I have chosen the following countries: the Netherlands, Germany, Sweden, Denmark, Norway, Great Britain and the United States. Although there are still large differences between these countries with respect to gay rights and gay cultures, and the road to these rights and subcultures was and is not easy everywhere, at least there *is* a gay culture compared to some African and Asian countries. Furthermore, these countries are accessible to me concerning their languages. As an overview of lesbian magazines published between 1924 and 2000 constitutes the first part of this research project, a definitive number of magazines cannot be mentioned here.

Research questions

The first part of the research concentrates on gaining an overview of all the lesbian magazines that have been published in the above-mentioned countries between 1924 and 2000. This will be possible with the help of IHLIA, which is an international gay/lesbian library, archive, information and documentation centre concerning homosexuality and sexual diversity.[8] It boasts the largest library collection on and by gay, lesbian, bisexual, transgender and queer people in the Netherlands and Europe.[9] The second part of the research concentrates on lesbian magazines as part of a cultural infrastructure. As we will see, the international differences are evident with respect to gay rights and the existence of gay subcultures. Because of these differences it will be interesting to focus on the existence of a network between lesbian magazines.

8 IHLIA stands for Internationaal Homo en Lesbisch Informatiecentrum en Archief.

9 http://www.ihlia.nl/dutch/zoeken_catalogi/tijdschrift; http://www.ihlia.nl/english/english, accessed August 1, 2012.

In her book *Golden Cables of Sympathy. The Transatlantic Sources of Nineteenth-Century Feminism* Margaret H. McFadden describes how women in Europe and North America created virtual communities over the course of the nineteenth century through various forms of communication, support and a shared ideology.[10] I want to see to what extent this applies to lesbian magazines. The main aim is to gain insight into this network and to see in what way there is interaction between the magazines. The following example demonstrates that a virtual network between lesbian magazines did exist. The first British lesbian periodical, *Arena Three*, utilised the American magazine *The Ladder* to spread word of its existence.[11]

In the second part of the study I will use a combination of network analysis and discourse analysis – in which the magazines as well as other documents (such as letters) play a role – to determine if there are contacts between the magazines and what they consist of. Martin Meeker has done research on networks that linked individuals to a larger field of social knowledge about homosexuality. One of the key innovations he points to in his *Contacts Desired. Gay and Lesbian Communications and Community, 1940s–1970s* is the mass media's treatment of homosexuals in the late 1950s and early 1960s. However, as he mainly focuses on the United States, insight into the nature of an international network is lacking.

It is imperative to take note of some additional issues. First of all, lesbian magazines exist in all shapes and sizes. They have different backgrounds, aims and features. Therefore, it is worth taking these differences into account, as well as how long each magazine existed and how often they were published. Furthermore, the magazines should be placed in a historical context. This means that the political, cultural and social situation between 1924 and 2000 must be taken into account. What kind of legislation was there and what did the homosexual subculture look like during these years? In other words, it is necessary to place the results of the study within a historical framework.

In Europe alone, the differences between sexual cultures is evident. This is apparent in both the homosexual subcultures and the political situation. Even before the Second World War, Berlin was home to a vibrant lesbian subculture and established itself as the gay and lesbian capital

10 Margaret H. McFadden, *Golden Cables of Sympathy. The Transatlantic Sources of Nineteenth-Century Feminism* (Lexington, 1999), inside book jacket.

11 Rupp, *Sapphistries*, p. 197.

between 1870 and 1940.[12] During the 1950s, gay life in Paris, Copenhagen and Amsterdam took off.[13] When we take a look at the political situation concerning gay rights on an international level we find obvious differences. In the Netherlands, for example, homosexual acts were decriminalised in 1811. In Sweden, however, such acts remained illegal until 1944.[14] These are only a few examples of the international differences concerning homosexuality. In this context and because there has been little research on lesbian magazines in particular and their role in cultural transfer and transmission, it would be interesting to take a closer look at their impact in this field.

12 Leila Rupp, 'Loving Women in the Modern World', in: Robert Aldrich, ed., *Gay Life and Culture: A World History* (London, 2006), p. 223.

13 Gert Hekma, 'The Gay World: 1980 to the Present', in: Aldrich, *Gay Life and Culture*, p. 333.

14 http://www.ihlia.nl/dutch/algemeen/Tijdbalk; http://www.rfsl.se/?p=413, accessed August 1, 2012.

Multicultural Literature: Exotic or Mainstream?

A Proposal for a Comparative Study of Swedish Multicultural Literature in Translation

« Ingeborg Kroon »

Since the Second World War, societies have become more multicultural. First, the war created refugee streams, and later the developing Western countries recruited guest workers. The differences in economic development led people from poorer countries to become established in richer countries. Against this background a 'multicultural culture' developed, and within literature, the genre of 'multicultural literature' (or 'migrant literature') arose, referring to literature written by authors with a partly or wholly foreign background. Many studies treat this type of literature from the point of view of one literary field or as belonging to a specific type of literature; however, the authors involved tend to not want to be placed in a specific group.

In this article I would like to make a proposal for a study of Swedish-language multicultural literature that has been translated into other languages. Studies of the reception of Dutch multicultural literature in other countries, for example, have already shown that there can be different opinions on the literature in these countries to those current in the Netherlands.[1] In relation to the Swedish literary field, it would be interesting to study how multicultural literature from Sweden is considered abroad. In describing the meaning of multicultural literature within this

1 In 2012 a book was published on the reception of the Dutch author Arnon Grunberg in Italy, Spain, Catalonia, Portugal and Romania. While a number of books by Grunberg have been translated into Italian, in Catalonia and Portugal only one book has been translated, which is at least partly related to the culture and opinions there. Dolores Ross, Arie Pos, Marleen Mertens, eds., *Ieder zijn eigen Arnon Grunberg. Vertaling, promotie en receptie in Italië, Spanje, Catalonië, Portugal en Roemenië* (Ghent/Tilburg/Utrecht, 2012).

proposed research project, I would like to use the work of the Swedish literary scholar Magnus Nilsson, who has written some of the most recent studies.[2] In relation to working-class literature he states that during periods when the working class is much discussed, for example because of changes occurring in society which concern them, there will probably be an accompanying influence on the reception of working-class literature.[3] My proposal concerns the period of migration after the Second World War and the effects on the reception of multicultural authors in the present at a time in which migration is such a divisive topic in the media, politics and society in general. I will examine multicultural literature considered as that written by authors with a partly or wholly foreign background who write in Swedish and who wish – probably because of the strong interest in society concerning migration – to be considered simply as authors.

Multicultural literature and Swedish literary theory

In Swedish literary theory, multicultural literature is widely discussed, with one subject of the scholarly discussion being the definition of the term and how literature written by authors with a partly or wholly foreign background should be considered. According to Nilsson, scholars can pay too much attention to ethnic identity and in doing so tend to use what he calls an 'ethnic filter'.[4] To support this point of view, he refers to the Swedish

2 Magnus Nilsson, 'Litteratur, etnicitet och föreställningen om det mångkulturella samhället', *Samlaren* 129 (2008), pp. 270-304.

3 Magnus Nilsson, *Den föreställda mångkulturen. Klass och etnicitet i svensk samtidsprosa* (Möklinta, 2010), p. 55.

4 Two scholars Nilsson mentions are Satu Gröndahl and Lars Wendelius, both of whom published studies on migrant literature in 2002. Gröndahl wrote about the ambiguity of the term 'migrant literature': sometimes a writer belongs to a quite new migrant group, sometimes to a minority group. Migrant literature is included in literary histories but only when it the work is written in Swedish, where it is mentioned under headings such as 'The new Swedes', and thus is distinguished from the major, norm-building literature and norm-giving term of 'writer'. Wendelius focused on writers living in Sweden but having non-Swedish origins and how they are viewed (in reviews). The books have themes that refer to belonging to an ethnic minority. Concerning literature reception, Wendelius analysed reviews and found that they focus on a writer's background, for example on the historical or political situation in their original homeland.

writer Astrid Trotzig, who was originally from South Korea but was adopted by Swedish parents.[5] Trotzig wrote an essay on how writers with a partly or wholly foreign background are viewed in Sweden and found that not all such writers are treated as migrant authors.[6] Nilsson argues that the ethnic filter is the product of a general perception about multicultural society and that to develop such an idea, another idea is needed first, that of a country – in this case Sweden – that was homogeneous in the past.[7] Culture, and especially ethnicity, has become a 'key' for understanding present society as being multicultural, and past society, which was a post-industrial society composed of different classes, as monocultural.[8] Nilsson links this to Pierre Bourdieu's theory of the cultural field and the notion of symbolic ethnicity: in this case 'exotic ethnicity' can be seen as cultural capital, and as a symbol of belonging to a particular, other culture. Accepting or refusing this capital can have consequences for the position of such authors within the literary field. Nilsson concludes that 'this results in writers with a non-Swedish ethnicity being offered authorial roles which consequently give them entry to certain positions within the literary field'.[9]

In addition to the Swedish scholars already mentioned, there are scholars from other countries who also study Swedish multicultural literature. The German scholar Wolfgang Behschnitt has devoted several studies to this subject and, according to his research, literature is a way with which the self-image of a country can be formulated.[10] Concerning readers' expectations, the background of the author plays an important role and '... [sind] die Biographie des Autors und der Bezug auf seinen Erfahrungshintergrund wesentliche (...) um einen Test dieser Kategorie

5 Ibidem, p. 15.

6 Astrid Trotzig, 'Makten över prefixen', in: Moa Matthis, ed., *Orientalism på svenska* (Stockholm, 2005), pp. 104-127.

7 Nilsson, *Litteratur*, p. 274.

8 Nilsson, *Den föreställda mångkulturen*, p. 60.

9 'Resultatet ... blir att författare med icke-svensk etnicitet erbjuds etnifierade författarroller som i sin tur ger tillträde till vissa positioner i det litterära fältet', Nilsson, *Litteratur*, p. 299.

10 Wolfgang Behschnitt and Thomas Mohnike, 'Interkulturelle Authentizität? Überlegungen zur "anderen". Ästhetik der schwedischen "invandrarlitteratur"', in: Wolfgang Behschnitt and Elisabeth Herrmann, eds., *Über Grenzen. Grenzgänge der Skandinavistik. Festschrift zum 65. Geburtstag von Heinrich Anz* (Würzburg, 2007), p. 83.

zuordnen zu können'.[11] However, semantic and moral considerations (the extra literary reality, the background – biography – of the author) may not be determining criteria. Therefore, Wolfgang Behschnitt proposes to consider the term 'migrant literature' as a kind of label '… unter der *Literatur* das diskursiv geforderte "Einwanderer-Attribut" ablegte und stattdessen soziale Wirklichkeit neu verhandelte'.[12] Ingeborg Kongslien (University of Oslo) is also of the opinion that the term is problematic. However, she thinks that it can still be useful for promoting literature, as in the cases of women's literature and working-class literature 'which enabled these literatures to carve out their own space in the literary field and to introduce new fields of reference'.[13] Kongslien considers migrant literature to be a part of contemporary Scandinavian literature and suggests that writers can contribute to the dynamics of multicultural societies.

Multicultural literature and the literary field

Regarding the transfer of literature, different factors and actors play a role within the literary field. Sociological theories concerning the interaction and relationships between these factors and actors have been developed, throwing light on different aspects. Field or system theories have been developed by Itamar Even-Zohar and Bourdieu, among others. Even-Zohar developed the notion of the polysystem,[14] which focuses on the text.[15] Internal and external factors can influence the structure of the field, as well as a dynamic struggle between the centre and periphery of the field to establish the best position for actors. Even-Zohar distinguishes six factors specifically related to the literary polysystem which are active and related to each other: the producer, the product, the institutions, the repertoire, the market and the consumers.[16] Bourdieu developed the theory of a field

11 Ibidem, p. 80.

12 Ibidem, p. 97.

13 Ingeborg Kongslien, 'Migrant or multicultural literature in the Nordic countries', *Eurozine* (2006), http://www.eurozine.com/articles/2006-08-03-kongslien-en.html.

14 Itamar Even-Zohar, 'Polysystem studies', *Poetics Today* 11 (1) (1990), pp. 34-44.

15 Michaela Wolf, 'Naar een sociologie van het vertalen', in: Ton Naaijkens et al., eds., *Denken over vertalen. Tekstboek vertaalwetenschap* (Nijmegen, 2004), p. 391.

16 Even-Zohar, 'Polysystem studies', pp. 34-44.

as an 'autonomous social universe'[17] with actors that occupy different positions and gain a certain power by acquiring economic, cultural or symbolic capital.[18]

The kind of capital can influence their positions and the field thus becomes a field of forces. Gisèle Sapiro and Johan Heilbron consider translating as a 'transnational transfer' with political, cultural and economic relationships between countries characterised by rivalry and competition,[19] which leads to unequal exchanges between countries. The larger a language, the more literature is exported; the smaller, the more translations are made.[20]

Proposal for research

Despite ongoing discussion in the Swedish literary field about literature by authors with a foreign background there is still no clear definition or a clear understanding of the position of migrant literature in Sweden. Concerning migrant literature in Germany, Barbara Fennell has distinguished three development phases: 1. The pre-literature phase, with literature about the loss of identity, often in short epic or poetic form, 2. Pre-literature becomes migrant literature, with the construction of a new identity and literature with more variable content and form but still about migrant themes, 3. Migrant literature becomes mainstream literature, with the consolidation of identity and the wish of the authors to be taken seriously as writers.[21] Sandra van Voorst has applied this scheme to the Dutch situation to analyse the position of the migrant writer Kader Abdolah.[22]

Within the framework of cultural transfer we can raise the question of how migrant literature is considered after translation. As Trotzig and

17 'autonome sociale universa', Pierre Bourdieu, *Opstellen over smaak, habitus en het veldbegrip*. Gekozen door Dick Pels (Amsterdam, 1989), p. 12.

18 Ibidem, pp. 120-144.

19 Gisèle Sapiro and Johan Heilbron, 'Outline for a Sociology of Translation. Current Issues and Future Prospects', in: Michaela Wolf and Alexandra Fukari, eds., *Constructing a Sociology of Translation* (Amsterdam, 2007), p. 95.

20 Ibidem, p. 96.

21 Barbara A. Fennell, *Language, Literature and the Negotiation of Identity: Foreign Worker German in the Federal Republic of Germany* (Chapel Hill/London, 1997), pp. 124-132.

22 Sandra van Voorst, 'Wordt vervolgd: de receptie van Nederlandse migrantenliteratuur', in: *Neerlandica extra muros* 45 (1) (2007), pp. 11-22.

Nilsson mentioned in their studies, not all authors are seen and judged to be migrant writers. For this study, two authors have been chosen who are considered as such and who write in Swedish and who have been translated into other languages: Theodor Kallifatides (born in Greece in 1938) and Jonas Hassen Khemiri (born in Sweden in 1978, Swedish mother and Tunisian father). The proposal is to study the reception and transfer of their work in different countries: in the large Western European countries of France and Germany, the Dutch-speaking area of Belgium and the Netherlands, and the Scandinavian countries of Denmark and Norway. An overview can be constructed based on the six different phases which Petra Broomans and Ester Jiresch have set out as the basis for their analysis of cultural transfer:[23] 1. The discovery and introduction of the author, 2. Quarantine phase of an author, in which a transmitter attempts to find a way to have their work published, 3. Translation, 4. Publication, 5. Reception (reviews in daily newspapers, etc.), 6. Post-publication reception. Further questions that play a role in this analysis are: When was the work published in Sweden and when in the target areas? Which factors play a role in publishing?[24] What do the reviews say about the two authors and their works, their backgrounds and the genre?

23 Petra Broomans and Esther Jiresch, 'The Invasion of Books', in: Petra Broomans and Esther Jiresch, eds., *The Invasion of Books in Peripheral Literary Fields. Transmitting Preferences and Images in Media, Networks and Translation* (Groningen, 2011), pp. 10-13.

24 Ingrid Wikén Bonde, 'Van het ene polysysteem naar het andere. De receptie van de Vijftigers in het Zweedse literaire veld', in: Petra Broomans et al., eds., *Object: Nederlandse literatuur in het buitenland. Methode: onbekend. Vormen van onderzoek naar de receptie van literatuur uit het Nederlandse taalgebied* (Groningen, 2006), pp. 125-150. Wikén Bonde claims that a number of specific factors should be considered when a literature is transferred from an 'intramural' field (the source field) to an 'extramural' field (the target field): the topics or needs of the target culture (for example, in relation to political, economic fields); the need to know something about different literatures; the different reception in the extramural field compared with the reception in the intramural field; and accident. Wikén Bonde writes about 'accident' in this regard, because if 'missionaries' from the intramural field (who think it is desirable to transfer the literature from their field to the extramural field) and helpers (people from the extramural field who by accident come into contact with the intramural literature and become interested) are not present at the right moment, there is no transfer.

Regarding the development of literature sketched by Fennell and Van Voorst, another sub-question arises: Could development phases be distinguished after translation in a target area? Therefore, Fennell's three-phase scheme could also be used to analyse how multicultural literature is considered and developed as pre-literature, migrant literature and mainstream literature. Such an approach could throw light on the development of migrant literature in a broader sense than just a source literary field. In this way this approach could show whether multicultural literature ultimately belongs to a mainstream literature or is seen as an exotic literature, thus supplementing earlier studies on multicultural literature.

About the Authors

Els Biesemans studied Dutch and Scandinavian literature and linguistics at Ghent University and received an MA in Comparative Modern Literature. Driven by a deep fascination for the turn of the nineteenth century, she wrote her Master's thesis about the representation of urbanity in Swedish literature from 1860 onwards. In 2008 she started work on a PhD, investigating the reception of Scandinavian literature in the Dutch-language area in the same period. The translators, the people who actually make the transfer of literature possible, are the main focus of her research. Their personal preferences, ideological and political orientations, personal contacts, engagement in the literary field and professional ambitions are investigated, with an emphasis on how they influence the selection of translated texts, as well as on the evolution of all of these criteria over time.

Petra Broomans is Associate Professor of Scandinavian Linguistics and Literatures at the University of Groningen and visiting professor at Ghent University. She is the coordinator of the project 'Scandinavian Literature in Europe around 1900: the Influence of Language Politics, Gender and Aesthetics' (2004-2010) and the initiator of Studies on Cultural Transfer and Transmission (CTaT), with an emphasis on women cultural transmitters, cultural transfer and transmission history and minor language areas (see also www.soctat.org). One of the related projects she is working on is the 'Bibliography of Swedish and Swedish-Finnish literature in Dutch translation (1491-2007)'. She is also editor-in-chief of the series Studies on Cultural Transfer and Transmission and secretary of the board of the International Association for Scandinavian Studies (IASS). For further information please visit her website: www.petrabroomans.net.

Coppélie Cocq is a researcher at HUMlab, Umeå University, Sweden. She has a PhD in Sámi Studies in the field of folklore. Her current research investigates how Sámi expressive culture emerges in digital environments in the contemporary context of cultural and linguistic revitalisation. Her research interests concern storytelling, folklore and minority studies.

Bo G. Ekelund is an Associate Professor of English at the Department of English, Stockholm University. He has published on the conditions of authorship in the US and on scenes of recognition in contemporary fiction. His current research deals with the field of translation in Sweden and with the construction of space in Anglophone Caribbean literature. The article included here is part of research on the internationalisation of Swedish higher education, funded by the Swedish Research Council.

Lars Kleberg is Professor Emeritus of Russian at Södertörn University. He has published numerous articles on Russian avant-garde culture, translation and Russian and Polish literature. His book *Starfall: A Triptych* has been translated into five languages. He has edited anthologies about the theory and practice of literary translation and is the founder and general editor of the Swedish Dictionary of Translators, *Svenskt översättarlexikon* (www.oversattarlexikon.se).

Cees Koster teaches Translation Studies and is coordinator of the MA in the Theory and Practice of Translation at Utrecht University. He has published widely on the Dutch translation history of the nineteenth and twentieth centuries, and is an editor of the Dutch journal on translation *Filter*. Currently he is working on a Dutch translation history and a biography of the Dutch translator, poet and critic Pé Hawinkels.

Ingeborg Kroon studied at the Maastricht School for Translation and Interpreting from 1999 to 2003 (with French as her main language). From 2003 to 2008 she studied Scandinavian languages and cultures (Swedish as her main language) at the University of Groningen. She has since published articles on Swedish literature and the Swedish literary field in various journals, including the *Scandinavian Newsletter* and *De Parelduiker*. She works as a freelance translator into and from Swedish and teaches Swedish for adults. She has also taught courses in Swedish literature at the University of Groningen and is currently working on a 'Bibliography of Swedish and Swedish-Finnish literature in Dutch translation (1491-2007)' with Petra Broomans.

Godelieve Laureys is full professor of Scandinavian Linguistics and Literature at Ghent University. She also holds a honorary professorship at Groningen University. Her main field of research is modern Scandinavian linguistics, but she has also done research on cultural transfer and on the image of Scandinavia in Europe, as encoded in texts and discourse. She has published several books and numerous articles in national and international journals on a wide range of Scandinavian subjects. She is the editor-in-chief of three bidirectional bilingual dictionaries for the language pairs Dutch-Swedish, Dutch-Danish and Dutch-Finnish. From 2008 she has been the Ghent coordinator for the Studies on Cultural Transfer and Transmission-project, run in cooperation with the universities of Groningen and Uppsala.

Marta Ronne received her PhD in Comparative Literature from the Department of Comparative Literature at Uppsala University, Uppsala, Sweden. Currently she is connected to The Hugo Valentin Centre, Uppsala University. Her doctoral thesis was on gender and Swedish university novels published between 1903 and 1943. She has published several articles on women's literature, the sociology of literature and culture. Her research also encompasses literary critique in Sweden, as she is working on a professional biography of Margit Abenius (1899-1970), one of the most prominent Swedish literary critics of the twentieth century. She has published articles on the subject in previous volumes of the Studies on Cultural Transfer and Transmission series. She also works as a literary critic for Swedish newspapers. Since 2004, Ronne has been the Uppsala coordinator for the Studies on Cultural Transfer and Transmission project, run in cooperation with the universities of Ghent and Groningen.

Karina Smits received her MA in Scandinavian Languages and Cultures from the University of Groningen and has also studied in Stockholm. In her BA thesis 'Selma Lagerlöf and the forbidden love' (2010), she discusses the extent to which both general histories of literature and histories of women's literature in particular, published in various years, wrote about Selma Lagerlöf's sexual orientation. Her MA thesis 'The clothes and buttons of the woman. Two Swedish literary biographies of Fredrika Bremer' (2012), functions as a case study for gaining insight into the development of literary biography. The two biographies of Fredrika Bremer (from 1896 and 2001) are compared from a female literary-historical perspective.

Liselotte Vandenbussche studied English and Dutch literature and linguistics at Ghent University and literary theory at KU Leuven. She completed her PhD in 2006 at the Centre for Gender Studies at Ghent University with a dissertation on liberal women writers in Flemish literary and cultural journals around 1900. It was published in 2008 as *Het veld der verbeelding. Vrijzinnige vrouwen in Vlaamse literaire en algemeen-culturele tijdschriften (1870-1914)* by the Royal Academy for Dutch Literature and Linguistics. She is currently a postdoctoral research assistant at the Department of Translation Studies of the University College Ghent and affiliated researcher at Ghent University. From September 2012 to February 2013 she will be working at the North-West University in Potchefstroom, South Africa. She has published work in a number of journals, including the *Tijdschrift voor Nederlandse Taal- en Letterkunde, Nederlandse Letterkunde, Spiegel der Letteren, Women's History Review, Western American Literature* and *The Translator*, and contributed to several books, with articles on gender, literature and translation in nineteenth and early twentieth-century Flanders.

Sandra van Voorst is an Assistant Professor of Modern Dutch Literature at the University of Groningen. She obtained her PhD in 1997 with the dissertation *Weten wat er te koop is. Vier Nederlandse uitgeverijen en hun vertaalde fondsen 1945-1970* ('Knowing what to buy. Four Dutch publishers and their translation funds, 1945-1970'). Her current research includes the professionalisation, internationalisation and politicisation of the Dutch literary field in the twentieth century. She has recently published articles on PEN Nederland (the Dutch PEN Club), the Vereniging 'Nederlandsche Vertalingen' (the Association for 'Dutch Translations') and the Stichting ter bevordering van de vertaling van Nederlands literair werk (Foundation for the Promotion of Dutch Literary Works).

Bibliography

Abenius, M., *Memoarer från det inre* (Stockholm, 1963).

Adkins, L. and Skeggs, B., *Feminism After Bourdieu* (Oxford, 2004).

Aerts, R., 'Het tijdschrift als culturele factor en als historische bron', *Groniek* 135 (1996), pp. 171-182.

Ahlström, G., *Det moderna genombrottet i Nordens litteratur* (Stockholm, 1974).

Alberdingk Thijm, P., 'Een woord van eendracht', *Het Belfort* 1 (1886), pp. 115-120.

Alliet, I. and Deridder, I., *Geschiedenis van de wetgeving in verband met het middelbaar onderwijs voor meisjes (1894-1962). Casus middelbare normaalschool Onze-Lieve-Vrouw-ten-Doorn Eeklo* (Master's thesis Ghent University, 2005).

Anaya, J., *The Situation of the Sami People in the Sápmi Region of Norway, Sweden and Finland. Report of the Special Rapporteur on the Situation of Human Rights and Fundamental Freedoms of Indigenous People* (2011). http://www.ohchr.org/Documents/Issues/IPeoples/SR/A-HRC-18-35-Add2_en.pdf

Andersson, H.-L., *Doxa och debatt* (Gothenburg, 2008).

Andringa, E., Levie, S. and Sanders, M., 'Het buitenland bekeken. Vijf internationale auteurs door Nederlandse ogen (1900-2000)', *Nederlandse Letterkunde* 3 (2006), pp. 197-210.

Arbetsmarknadsdepartementet, *Lag om nationella minoriteter och minoritetsspråk* (Stockholm, 2009).

Bakhtin, M., *The Dialogic Imagination*, translated by Caryl Emerson and Michael Holquist (Austin, 1981).

Bakhtin, M., *Det dialogiska ordet*, translated by Johan Öberg (Stockholm, 1988).

Balto, A., 'Upbringing for Self-esteem, Zest for Life and Joy', in: *Woman in a Northern Landscape* (Nordfold, 1999).

Balto, A., *Samisk barneoppdragelse i endring* (Oslo, 1997).

Barthes, R., *Image – Music – Text* (New York, 1977).

Basso, K.H., *Wisdom Sits in Places: Landscape and Language Among the Western Apache* (Albuquerque, 1996).

Bauman, R., *Story, Performance and Event. Contextual Studies of Oral Narrative* (Cambridge, 1986).

Behschnitt, W. and Mohnike, T., 'Interkulturelle Authentizität? Überlegungen zur "anderen". Ästhetik der schwedischen "invandrarlitteratur"', in: Behschnitt, W. and Herrmann, E., eds., *Über Grenzen. Grenzgänge der Skandinavistik. Festschrift zum 65. Geburtstag von Heinrich Anz* (Würzburg, 2007), pp. 79-100.

Belpaire, M.-E., 'Boekennieuws. J. Destrée over het talenvraagstuk in België', *Dietsche Warande en Belfort* 24 (1924), pp. 474-477.

Ben-Amos, D., 'Toward a Definition of Folklore in Context', *The Journal of American Folklore* 84 (331) (1971), pp. 3-15.

Biesemans, E., Vertalers van Scandinavische literatuur naar het Nederlands tussen 1860 en 1940. Evolutie van de samenstelling van de groep van vertalers en hun ideologische, maatschappelijke en professionele voorkeuren, 2013 (doctoral dissertation, in print).

Birkeland, K., *Samiska sagor: 25 sydsamiska sagor* (Stockholm, 1988).

Bjørnson, B., *De moderne Noorsche literatuur* (Leiden, 1896), translated by M. Meyboom of the original 'Den moderne norske literatur', in: *Artikler og taler* (Copenhagen, 1896), pp. 305-330.

Boas, F., *Geographical Names of the Kwakiutl Indians* (New York, 1934).

Boissevain, J., *Friends of Friends: Networks, Manipulators and Coalitions* (Oxford, 1974).

Bolckmans, A., *From Nordic Folk Tales to Science Fiction* (Ghent, 1988).

Bourdieu, P., *Opstellen over smaak, habitus en het veldbegrip*. Gekozen door Dick Pels (Amsterdam, 1989).

Bourdieu, P., *Homo Academicus* (Stanford, 1988).

Brandes, G., *Hovedstrømninger i det 19de aarhundredes litteratur* (Copenhagen, 1872).

Brants, M., *De hervorming van het middelbaar onderwijs* (Ghent, 1906).

Briggs, C.L., *Competence in Performance: the Creativity of Tradition in Mexican Verbal Art* (Philadelphia, 1988).

Broady, D. and Palme, M., 'Inträdet. Om litteraturkritik som intellektuellt fält', in: Broady, D., ed., *Kulturens fält* (Gothenburg, 1998), pp. 173-215.

Broomans, P., 'Zichtbaar in de canon. Spelregels voor cultuurbemiddelaars', *Tijdschrift voor Nederlandse Taal- en Letterkunde* 128 (3-4) (2012, forthcoming), pp. 72-91.

Broomans, P. and Jiresch, E., 'The Invasion of Books', in: Broomans, P. and Jiresch, E., eds., *The Invasion of Books in Peripheral literary Fields. Transmitting Preferences and Images in Media, Networks and Translation* (Groningen, 2011), pp. 9-22.

Broomans, P. and Jiresch, E., eds., *The Invasion of Books in Peripheral Literary Fields. Transmitting Preferences and Images in Media, Networks and Translation* (Groningen, 2011).

Broomans, P. and Ronne, M., 'In the Vanguard of Cultural Transfer', in: Broomans, P. and Ronne, M., eds., *In the Vanguard of Cultural Transfer. Cultural Transmitters and Authors in Peripheral Literary Fields* (Groningen, 2010), pp. 1-12.

Broomans, P. and Ronne, M., eds., *In the Vanguard of Cultural Transfer. Cultural Transmitters and Authors in Peripheral Literary Fields* (Groningen, 2010).

Broomans, P., 'Preface', in: Broomans, P., ed., *From Darwin to Weil. Women as Transmitters of Ideas* (Groningen, 2009), pp. VII-VIII.

Broomans, P., 'Introduction: Women as Transmitters of Ideas', in: Broomans, P., ed., *From Darwin to Weil. Women as Transmitters of Ideas* (Groningen, 2009), pp. 1-20.

Broomans, P., ed., *From Darwin to Weil. Women as Transmitters of Ideas* (Groningen, 2009).

Broomans, P., 'Den nordiska litteraturens fälttåg i Europa kring 1900. Om Brandes och medresenärer, maktkamp och avfall', in: Harsløf, O., ed., *Georg Brandes og Europa* (Copenhagen, 2004), pp. 163-176.

Broomans, P., '"Vertalingen waar haast bij is, boeken die gerecenseerd moeten worden". Dien Logeman-Van der Willigen', *Spieghel Historiael* 42 (2002), pp. 47-66.

Broomans, P., *Detta är jag. Stina Aronsons litteraturhistoriska öde* (Stockholm, 2001).

Broomans, P., 'In the name of God and the Father. Scandinavian women's literary history from a meta-literary historical point of view', in: Van Dijk, S., Van Gemert, L. and Ottway, S., eds., *Writing the History of Women's Writing. Towards an international approach*, Koninklijke Nederlandse Akademie van Wetenschappen Verhandelingen, Afd. Letterkunde, Nieuwe Reeks, deel 182 (Amsterdam, 2001), pp. 125-134.

Broomans, P., 'Scandia i Nederländerna. Om Margaretha Meijboom och hennes nordiska tidskrifter', *TijdSchrift voor Skandinavistiek* 22 (1) (2001), pp. 155-167.

Burke, P. and Po-Chia Hsia, R., eds., *Cultural Translation in Early Modern Europe* (Cambridge, 2007).

Burke, P., *Lost (and Found) in Translation: A Cultural History of Translators and Translating in Early Modern Europe* (Wassenaar, 2005).

Casanova, P., *The World Republic of Letters* (Cambridge, Mass., 2004).

Casanova, P., *La république mondiale des lettres* (Paris, 1999).

Christensson, J., ed., *Signums svenska kulturhistoria*, 1–8 (Lund/ Stockholm, 2004–2009).

Christiansen, R.T., *The Migratory Legends: a Proposed List of Types with a Systematic Catalogue of the Norwegian Variants* (Helsinki, 1958).

Classe, O., *Encyclopedia of Literary Translation into English* (London, 2000).

Clifford, J., *Routes: Travel and Translation in the Late Twentieth Century* (Cambridge, 1997).

Cocq, C., 'Anthropological Places, Digital Spaces and Imaginary Spaces', *Folklore* 124 (forthcoming, 2013).

Cocq, C., *Revoicing Sámi Narratives. North Sámi Storytelling at the Turn of the 20th Century* (Umeå, 2008).

Cocq, C., 'Stállu - Återkomsten. En jämförelse av traditionella berättelser i dåtid och nutid', in: Axelsson, P. and Sköld, P., eds., *Ett land, ett folk. Sápmi i historia och nutid*, vol. 3 (Umeå, 2005), pp. 273-284.

Cruikshank, J., 'Getting the Words Right: Perspectives on Naming and Places in Athapaskan Oral History', *Arctic Anthropology* 27 (1) (1990), pp. 52-65.

De Korne, H., 'Indigenous Language Education Policy: Supporting Community-Controlled Immersion in Canada and the US', *Language Policy* 9 (2010), pp. 115-141.

Delabastita, D., 'From Aesop to Zweig and From Martial to Martial Arts Fiction: Charting the History of Literary Translation into English', *Target* 1 (2002), pp. 149-171.

Demoor, M., *Their Fair Share. Women, Power and Criticism in the Atheneum, from Millicent Garett Fawcett to Katherine Mansfield, 1870-1920* (Aldershot, 2000).

Derrida, J., *Of Grammatology*, translated by Gayatri Spivak (Baltimore, 1974).

Derrida, J., *Positions* (Chicago, 1981).

De Schryver, R., 'Marie Elisabeth Belpaire', in: De Schryver, R. et al., eds., *Nieuwe encyclopedie van de Vlaamse Beweging* (Tielt, 1998), pp. 457-458.

Dijkman, A., *Opzij & aan de kant met haar. De constructie van norm en afwijking in Opzij tussen 1972 en 2002* (Nijmegen, 2008).

Dimock, W.-C., *Through Other Continents: American Literature Across Deep Time* (Princeton, 2008).

Dolan, B., *Ladies of the Grand Tour. British Women in Pursuit of Enlightenment and Adventure in Eighteenth-Century Europe* (New York, 2001).

Dooms, B., *Een gezonde noordervorst. Vlaamse visies op Noorse literatuur tussen 1830 en 1914* (Kapellen, 2001).

DuBois, T.A., 'Insider and Outsider: An Inari Saami Case', *Scandinavian Studies* 67 (1) (1995), pp. 63-76.

Ekelund, A., *Julia Kristevas genomslag i Sverige – fransk feminism som symbolisk tillgång i litteraturkritikens fält* (Uppsala, 2011).
Ekman, H.-G., *Humor, grotesk och pikaresk: studier i Lars Ahlins realism* (Staffanstorp, 1975).
Elenius, L., *Nationalstat och minoritetspolitik. Samer och finskspråkiga minoriteter i ett jämförande nordiskt perspektiv* (Lund, 2006).
Engdahl, H., *Den romantiska texten: en essä i nio avsnitt* (Stockholm, 1986).
Eriksen, T.H., *Ethnicity and Nationalism: Anthropological Perspectives* (London, 1993).
Espagne, M., 'Jenseits der Komparatistik. Zur Methode der Erforschung von Kulturtransfers', in: Mölk, U., ed., *Europäische Kulturzeitschriften um 1900 als Medien transnationaler und transdisziplinärer Wahrnehmung* (Abhandlungen der Akademie der Wissenschaften zu Göttingen, Philologisch-Historische Klasse, Dritte Folge, Bd. 273) (Göttingen, 2006), pp. 13-32.
Even-Zohar, I., 'Polysystem studies', *Poetics Today* 11 (1) (1990), pp. 39-44.
Ezell, M.J.M., *Writing Women's Literary History* (Baltimore, 1993).
Fennell, B.A., *Language, Literature and the Negotiation of Identity: Foreign Worker German in the Federal Republic of Germany* (Chapel Hill/London, 1997).
Fienup-Riordan, A., ed., *Qaluyaarmiuni Nunamtenek Qanemciput/ Our Nelson Island Stories: Meanings of Place of the Bering Sea Coast*, translated by Alice Rearden (Seattle, 2011).
Fjellström, P., *Samernas samhälle i tradition och nutid* (Stockholm, 1986).
Foz, C., 'Translation, History and the Translation Scholar', in: Bastin, G.L. and Bandia, P.F., eds., *Charting the Future of Translation History* (Ottawa, 2006), pp. 131-144.
France, P. and Gillespie, S., eds., *The Oxford History of Literary Translation in English*, vol. 1: *To 1550* (Oxford, 2008); vol. 2: *1550–1660* (Oxford, 2010); vol. 3: *1660–1790* (Oxford, 2005); vol. 4: *1790–1900* (Oxford, 2006).
France, P., 'Introduction', in: France, P. ed., *The Oxford Guide to Literature in English Translation* (Oxford, 2000), pp. xix-xxii.
France, P., ed., *The Oxford Guide to Literature in English Translation* (Oxford, 2000).
Frykman, J. and Löfgren, O., *Den kultiverade människan* (Lund, 1979).
Grave, J., *Zulk vertalen is een werk van liefde. Bemiddelaars van Nederlandstalige literatuur in Duitsland 1890-1914* (Nijmegen, 2001).
Grenoble, L.A. and Whaley, L.J., *Saving Languages: An Introduction to Language Revitalization* (Cambridge, 2006).

Grit, D.C., 'Recensie: Bart Dooms, Een gezonde noordervorst. Vlaamse visies op Noorse literatuur tussen 1830 en 1914', *TijdSchrift voor Skandinavistiek* 23 (2) (2002), pp. 295-300.

Grit, D.C., *Driewerf zalig Noorden. Over literaire betrekkingen tussen de Nederlanden en Scandinavië* (Maastricht, 1994).

Grit, D.C., 'Vlaams Scandinavisme en Stijn Streuvels', *Spiegel der Letteren* 33 (3) (1991), pp. 149-170.

Gröndahl, S., *Litteraturens gränsland. Invandrar- och minoritetslitteratur i nordiskt perspektiv* (Uppsala, 2002).

Gustavsson, M., 'Litteraturteorins expansion. Svenska doktorsavhandlingar i litteraturvetenskap 1976-1985', in: Landgren, B., ed., *Universitetsämne i brytningstider* (Uppsala, 2005).

Hamelius, P., 'Boekbeoordeling', *Vlaanderen* 2 (1904), pp. 478-486.

Hammarsköld, L., *Svenska vitterheten. Historiskt-kritiska anteckningar* (Stockholm, 1833).

Hamsun, K., 'Die literarische Bewegung in Norwegen', *Aus fremden Zungen* 4 (1894), pp. 55-56, 102-104, 151-152.

Hamsun, K., 'Le Mouvement littéraire en Norvège', *Revue des revues* 7 (1893), pp. 721-727, 801-806.

Hansen, C.J., *Noordsche Letteren* (Ghent, 1860).

Hansen, C.J., *Reisbrieven uit Dietschland en Denemark* (Ghent, 1860).

Hartmann, G., *Criticism in the Wilderness* (New Haven, 1980).

Heilbron, J., 'Het wereldvertaalstelsel', *Filter* 7 (2000), pp. 38-44.

Hekma, G., 'The Gay World: 1980 to the Present', in: Aldrich, R., ed., *Gay Life and Culture: A World History* (London, 2006), pp. 333-363.

Holmberg, C.-G. and Ljung, P.E., eds., *Översättning - adaption, interpretation, transformation: IASS 2010 proceedings: föredrag vid den 28:e studiekonferensen i International Association of Scandinavian Studies (IASS) i Lund 3-7 augusti 2010*, http://nile.lub.lu.se/ojs/index.php/IASS2010.

Hutcheon, L. and Valdés, M.J., 'Theorizing Literary History in Dialogue', in: Hutcheon, L. and Valdés, M.J., eds., *Rethinking Literary History. A Dialogue on Theory* (Oxford, 2002), pp. IX-XIII.

Ingold, T., 'Conversations from the North', in: Kaankanpää, P. et al., eds., *Knowledge and power in the Arctic: Proceedings at a Conference in Rovaniemi 16-18 April 2007* (Rovaniemi, 2007), pp. 11-15.

Ingold, T., *The Perception of Environment: Essays on Livelihood, Dwelling and Skill* (London, 2000).

Ingwersen, N., 'The Need for Narrative: The Folktale as Response to History', *Scandinavian Studies* 67 (1) (1995), pp. 77-90.

Integrations- och jämställdhetsdepartementet, *Från erkännande till egenmakt - regeringens strategi för de nationella minoriteterna* (Stockholm, 2008/2009).

Jiresch, E., *The Role of Networks in the Work of Female Cultural Transmitters of Scandinavian Literature and Culture in Europe around 1900. A Comparative Study of the Dutch/Flemish Side and the Austrian/German Speaking Regions* (forthcoming).

Jiresch, E., 'Marie-Elisabeth Belpaire and Dina Logeman-Van der Willigen. Two cultural Transmitters in Flanders – in the Same Literary Field?', in: Broomans, P. and Ronne, M., eds., *In the Vanguard of Cultural Transfer. Cultural Transmitters and Authors in Peripheral Literary Fields* (Groningen, 2010), pp. 33-54.

Kalinowski, I., 'La vocation au travail de la traduction', *Actes de la recherche en sciences sociales* 144 (3) (2002), pp. 47-54.

Kleberg, L., ed., *Med andra ord. Texter om litterär översättning* (repr. Stockholm, 2010).

Kleberg, L., 'Att göra översättningar synliga. Om översättningshistoria och databasen Svenskt översättarlexikon', in: Jansson, E., ed., *En bok om böcker och bibliotek tillägnad Louise Brunes* (Huddinge, 2009), pp. 173-186.

Kleberg, L., ed., *Konsten att översätta. Föreläsningar vid Södertörns högskolas översättarseminarium 1998-2008* (Huddinge, 2008).

Klinkenberg, J.-M., 'De Franse literatuur in Vlaanderen', in: Rutten, M. and Weisgerber, J., eds., *Van Arm Vlaanderen tot De voorstad groeit* (Antwerp, 1988), pp. 517-529.

Klok, J., 'Greta Baars-Jelgersma, Cora Sandel and the Dutch Literary Field, 1925-1950. Aspects of Cross-national Literary Transfer', in: Broomans, P. and Ronne, M., eds., *In the Vanguard of Cultural Transfer. Cultural Transmitters and Authors in Peripheral Literary Fields* (Groningen, 2010), pp. 55-88.

Kongslien, I., 'Migrant or multicultural literature in the Nordic countries', *Eurozine* (2006), http://www.eurozine.com/articles/2006-08-03-kongslien-en.html.

Koster, C. and Naaijkens, T., 'Translators in Translation History – The Dutch Case'. Paper presented to The Fifth Biennial Conference of the American Translation & Interpreting Studies Association 'The Sociological Turn in Translation and Interpreting Studies'. April 24th, 2010.

Koster, C., 'Fame and Fortune in the Field of Shakespeare Translation: the Case of A.S. Kok', in: Toremans, T. and Verschueren, W., eds., *Crossing Cultures. Nineteenth-Century Anglophone Literature in the Low Countries* (Leuven, 2009), pp. 21-34.

Koster, C., 'Inleiding', in: Koster, C., ed., *Tussen roem en vergetelheid. Terug naar de negentiende eeuw, Filter* 14 (3) (2007), pp. 3-4.

Koster, C., *De Hollandsche Vertaalmolen. Nederlandse beschouwingen over vertalen, 1820-1885*. Reeks Vertaalhistorie, deel 5a (Den Haag, 2002).

Kuitert, L., *Het ene boek in vele delen. De uitgave van literaire series in Nederland 1850–1900* (Amsterdam, 1993).

Kulonen, U.-M., Seurujaärvi-Kari, I. and Pulkkinen, R., eds., *The Saami: a Cultural Encyclopaedia* (Helsinki, 2005).

Kvist, R., 'The Racist Legacy in Modern Swedish Saami Policy', *Canadian Journal of Native Studies* 14 (2) (1994), pp. 203-220.

Kvist, R., 'Swedish Saami Policy 1550-1990', in: Kvist, R., ed., *Readings in Saami History, Culture and Language III* (Umeå, 1992).

Lafarga, F. and Pegenaute, L., eds., *Historia de la traducción en España* (Salamanca, 2004).

Lagercrantz, E., *Lappische Volksdichtung*, vol. II (Helsinki, 1958).

Landzelius, K., ed., *Native on the Net: Indigenous and Diasporic Peoples in the Virtual Age* (London, 2006).

Laureys, G., 'Languages Policy as a Cornerstone of Nation-Building. Linguistic Identities in the Nordic Countries', in: Broomans, P. et al., eds., *The Beloved Mothertongue. Ethnolinguistic Nationalism in Small Nations: Inventories and Reflections* (Leuven, 2008), pp. 79-91.

Leavy, B., 'Digital Songlines: Digitising the Arts, Culture and Heritage Landscape of Aboriginal Australia', in: Dyson, L.E., Hendriks, M. and Grant, S., eds., *Information Technology and Indigenous People* (Hershey, 2007), pp. 159-169.

Leppihalme, R., Review of Riikonen, H.K., Kovala, U., Kujamäki, P. and Palaposki, O., eds., *Suomennoskirjallisuuden historia* 1–2 (Helsinki, 2007), *Across Languages and Cultures* 1 (2008), pp. 139-144.

Ljung, P.E., ed., *Transformationer: valda texter från International Association of Scandinavian Studies (IASS) 28:e konferens i Lund 2010* (Lund, 2011).

Logeman-van der Willigen, D., 'Een dag te Trondhjem', *De Week* 2 (1911), pp. 1-3.

Logeman-van der Willigen, D., 'Fridthjof Nansen', *De Week* 2 (1910), pp. 8-9.

Logeman-van der Willigen, D., 'Uit Noorwegen', *De Vlaamsche Gids* 6 (1910), pp. 320-327.

Logeman-van der Willigen, D., 'Scandinavische Kroniek', *De Vlaamsche Gids* 5 (1909), pp. 279-288.

Logeman-van der Willigen, D., 'Gustaf Siösteen: "Det moderna Belgien". Iakttagelser och Studier', *De Vlaamsche Gids* 4 (1908), pp. 94-96.

Logeman-van der Willigen, D., 'Holger Drachmann', *De Vlaamsche Gids* 4 (1908), pp. 187-192.
Logeman-van der Willigen, D., 'Jongere krachten in de moderne Noorsche literatuur', *De Vlaamsche Gids* 4 (1908), pp. 77-93.
Logeman-van der Willigen, D., 'Scandinavische Kroniek', *De Vlaamsche Gids* 2 (1906), pp. 274-281.
Lönnroth, L. and Delblanc, S., eds., *Den svenska litteraturen* I-VII (Stockholm, 1987-1990).
Lundmark, L., *Stulet land: svensk makt på samisk mark* (Stockholm, 2008).
Macherey, P., *In a Materialist Way: Selected Essays* (London, 1998).
Marcus, G. and Sollors, W., eds., *A New Literary History of America* (Cambridge, Mass., 2009).
McFadden, M.H., *Golden Cables of Sympathy. The Transatlantic Sources of Nineteenth-Century Feminism* (Lexington, 1999).
Meeker, M., *Contacts Desired. Gay and Lesbian Communications and Community, 1940s–1970s* (Chicago/London, 2006).
Meidal, B., *August Strindberg. Ursvensk och europé* (Stockholm, 1999).
Meyboom, M., 'Skandinavische literatuur in Nederland', *De Boekzaal* 05 (1911), pp. 45-49.
Moi, T., 'Appropriating Bourdieu. Feminist Theory and Pierre Bourdieu's Sociology of Culture', *New Literary History* 4 (1991), pp. 1017-1049.
Monié, K., *Ord som himlen når. Carl August Hagberg – En levnadsteckning* (Stockholm, 2008).
Moretti, F., *Graphs, Maps, Trees: Abstract Models for Literary History* (London, 2005).
Moretti, F., 'Conjectures on World Literature', *New Left Review* 1 (2000), pp. 54-68.
Myrhaug, M.-L., *I modergudinnens fotspor. Samisk religion med vekt pa kvinnelige kultutøvere og gudinnekult* (Oslo, 1997).
Nilsson, M., *Den föreställda mångkulturen. Klass och etnicitet i svensk samtidsprosa* (Möklinta, 2010).
Nilsson, M., 'Litteratur, etnicitet och föreställningen om det mångkulturella samhället', *Samlaren* 129 (2008), pp. 270-304.
Nolin, B., *Den gode europén. Studier i Georg Brandes' idéutveckling 1871-1893 med speciell hänsyn till hans förhållande till tysk, engelsk, slavisk och fransk litteratur* (Stockholm, 1965).
O'Brien, J., 'Toward a Reconstitution of Ethnicity: Capitalist Expansion and Cultural Dynamics in Sudan', *American Anthropologist* 88 (1986), pp. 898-906.

O'Dell, T. and Billing, P., *Experiencescapes: Tourism, Culture, and Economy* (Copenhagen, 2005).
Öhngren, B., *Litteraturforskningen i Sverige 1989-1996. En evaluering* (Stockholm, 2000).
Pease, D., 'New Americanists: Revisionist Interventions into the Canon', *Boundary* 2 (17) (1990), pp. 1-37.
Perkins, D., *Is Literary History Possible?* (Baltimore/London, 1992).
Pietikäinen, S., 'Broadcasting Indigenous Voices: Sami Minority Media Production', *European Journal of Communication* 23 (2) (2008), pp. 173-191.
Pietikäinen, S., 'Sami in Media: Questions of Language Vitality and Cultural Hybridisation', *Journal of Multicultural Discourses* 3 (1) (2008), pp. 22-35.
Pirak, A., *Jåhttee saamee viessoom* (Uppsala, 1937).
Pym, A., 'Humanizing Translation History', *Hermes – Journal of Language and Communication Studies* 42 (2009), pp. 23-48.
Pym, A., 'Two Principles, One Probable Paradox and a Humble Suggestion, All Concerning Translation Rates into Various Languages, Particularly English' (1999), http://www.tinet.cat/~apym/on-line/translation/rates/rates.html.
Pym, A., *Method in Translation History* (Manchester, 1998).
Qvigstad, J.K., *Lappiske eventyr och sagn I-IV* (Oslo, 1927-1929).
Regnér, G., *Försök til metriske öfversättningar från forntidens skalder. Med förutgående afhandling i samma ämne* (Stockholm, 1801).
Reymenants, G., 'Catholicism as a Stepping Stone to Authorship. The Contribution of Women to the Flemish Catholic Periodical *Dietsche Warande en Belfort*', in: Broomans, P., ed., *From Darwin to Weil. Women as Transmitters of Ideas* (Groningen, 2009), pp. 121-137.
Reymenants, G., *Vrouweninvloed in het literaire veld. De medewerking van vrouwen aan katholieke Vlaamse tijdschriften, weekbladen en kranten* (Ghent, 2005).
Riikonen, H.K., Kovala, U., Kujamäki, P. and Palaposki, O., eds., *Suomennoskirjallisuuden historia* 1–2 (Helsinki, 2007).
Ronne, M., 'Läsandets ambassadör. (forthcoming, 2013).
Ronne, M., '"There is Always an Invisible Reader..." The Swedish Critic Margit Abenius and the Making of a Female Cultural Transmitter', in: Broomans, P. and Ronne, M., eds., *In the Vanguard of Cultural Transfer. Cultural Transmitters and Authors in Peripheral Literary Fields* (Groningen, 2010), pp. 89-117.

Ronne, M., 'Decoding a Genius Mind – The French Philosopher Simone Weil (1909-1943) and the Swedish Critic Margit Abenius (1899-1970): a Case of Cultural Transmission', in: Broomans, P., ed., *From Darwin to Weil. Women as Transmitters of Ideas* (Groningen, 2009), pp. 139-157.

Roos, J.P. and Rotkirch, A., 'Fält i skuggan av fält; sensocialismens dubbelliv', in: Broady, D., ed., *Kulturens fält. En antologi* (Gothenburg, 1998), pp. 453-466.

Ross, D., Pos, A. and Mertens, M., eds., *Ieder zijn eigen Arnon Grunberg. Vertaling, promotie en receptie in Italië, Spanje, Catalonië, Portugal en Roemenië* (Ghent/Tilburg/Utrecht, 2012).

Rupp, L.J., *Sapphistries. A Global History of Love between Women* (New York/London, 2009).

Rupp, L.J., 'Loving Women in the Modern World', in: Aldrich, R., ed., *Gay Life and Culture: A World History* (London, 2006), pp. 223-247.

Russ, J., 'Anomalousness' and 'Aesthetics', in: Warhol, R.R. and Price Herndel, D., eds., *Feminisms. An Anthology of Literary Theory and Criticism* (New Brunswick/New Jersey, 1991), pp. 194-211.

Sapiro, G. and Heilbron, J., 'Outline for a Sociology of Translation. Current Issues and Future Prospects', in: Wolf, M. and Fukari, A., eds., *Constructing a Sociology of Translation* (Amsterdam, 2007), pp. 93-107.

Saressalo, L., 'The Threat from Without', in: Ahlbäck, T., ed., *Saami Religion* (Åbo, 1987), pp. 251-257.

Schenkeveld-van der Dussen, M.A. et al., eds., *Nederlandse literatuur, een geschiedenis* (Groningen, 1993).

Schück, H. and Warburg, K., eds., *Illustrerad svensk litteraturhistoria* (Stockholm, 1926-1932, ^{3}1985).

Sela-Sheffy, R., 'How to Be a (Recognized) Translator. Rethinking Habitus, Norms, and the Field of Translation', *Target* 17 (2005), pp. 1-26.

Sela-Sheffy, R., 'Canon Formation Revisited: Canon and Cultural Production', *Neohelicon* 29 (2002), pp. 141-159.

Servaes, J., *Communication for Development: One World, Multiple Cultures* (Cresskill, 1999).

Simon, S., *Gender in Translation. Cultural Identity and the Politics of Transmission* (London/New York, 1996).

Simons, L., *Vlaamse en Nederduitse literatuur in de 19de eeuw. II. Vertalingen, receptie, beïnvloeding* (Ghent, 1985).

Simons, L., 'Vlaams-Nederduitse betrekkingen in de 19e eeuw', in: Simons, L., *Oostnoordoost. Facetten van de uitstraling van Vlaanderens taal en literatuur* (Antwerp, 1969), pp. 27-48.

Sniader Lanser, S. and Torton Beck, E., '[Why] Are There No Great Women Critics? And What Difference Does It Make?', in: Sherman, J.A. and Torton Beck, E., eds., *The Prism of Sex. Essays on the Sociology of Knowledge* (Madison, 1979), pp. 79-91.

Sosnoski, J.J., *Token Professionals and Master Critics: A Critique of Orthodoxy in Literary Studies* (Albany, 1994).

Stark, S., *'Behind Inverted Commas'. Translation and Aglo-German Cultural Relations in the Nineteenth Century* (Clevedon, 1999).

Stenberg, L., *I kärlekens namn. Om människosynen, den nya kvinnan och framtidens samhälle i fem litteraturdebatter 1881-1909* (Stockholm, 2009).

Stoor, K., 'Bakhållet vid Lappskottbacken. En berättelse om "de främmande" i en samisk miljö', in: Kusmenko, J., ed., *The Sámi and the Scandinavians. Aspects of 2000 Years of Contact* (Hamburg, 2004), pp. 73-87.

SVT *Sápmi, Stálu čalbmi* (2002).

SVT *Sápmi, Stállu ja garjá* (1997).

Tigerstedt, E.N., ed., *Ny illustrerad svensk litteraturhistoria* (Stockholm, 1955–1957).

Trotzig, A., 'Makten över prefixen', in: Matthis, M., ed., *Orientalism på svenska* (Stockholm, 2005), pp. 104-127.

Trotzig, B., 'Till översättningens lov', *Dialoger* 33 (1995), pp. 7-9.

Turi, J., *An Account of the Sámi* (Chicago, 2011).

Turi, J., *Muittalus Samid Birra* (Stockholm, 1910).

Valdés, M.J., 'Rethinking the History of Literary History', in: Hutcheon, L. and Valdés, M.J., eds., *Rethinking Literary History. A Dialogue on Theory* (Oxford, 2002), pp. 63-115.

Van den Berg, W., 'Nederlandse romantiek, een verschijnsel in de marge?', *De Gids* 2 (1990), pp. 126-135.

Van den Berg, W., 'Romantiek in de Nederlandse letterkunde', in: Van Bork, G.J. and Laan, N., *Twee eeuwen literatuurgeschiedenis. Poëticale opvattingen in de Nederlandse literatuur* (Groningen, 1986), pp. 44-54.

Vandenbussche, L., 'The Import of English Literature by Women Translators in Flanders, 1870-1914. A Comparative Survey', in: Toremans, T. and Verschueren, W., eds., *Crossing Cultures. Nineteenth-Century Anglophone Literature in the Low Countries* (Leuven, 2009), pp. 137-154.

Vandenbussche, L., Vandermassen, G., Demoor, M. and Braeckman, J., 'Virginie Loveling (1836-1923) as a Cultural Mediator: From Translating Klaus Groth to Manipulating Charles Darwin', in: Broomans, P., ed., *From Darwin to Weil. Women as Cultural Transmitters of Ideas* (Groningen, 2009), p. 47-71.

Vandenbussche, L., *Het veld der verbeelding. Vrijzinnige vrouwen in Vlaamse literaire en algemeen-culturele tijdschriften (1870-1914)* (Ghent, 2008).

Van der Veen, E., 'De Nederlandse homo-pers: historie, omvang en bereik', in: Bakker, E. and Schuyf, J., eds., *Homoseksualiteit en de media. Verslag van een studiedag georganiseerd door Homo RTV Urania en Homostudies Utrecht* (Utrecht, 1985), pp. 59-86.

Van der Weel, A., 'Nineteenth-Century Literary Translations from English in a Book Historical Context', in: De Clercq, M., Toremans T. and Verschueren W., eds., *Textual Mobility and Cultural Transmission = Tekstmobiliteit en culturele overdracht* (Leuven, 2006), pp. 27-40.

Van Dijk, S., 'Een database voor het literair-historisch onderzoek naar schrijfsters: "Women Writers before 1900"', *Muzen aan het werk. Jaarboek voor vrouwengeschiedenis* (2003), pp. 210-216.

Van Dijk, S., 'Schrijfsters vóór 1900 en hun internationale context: een database als hulpmiddel voor de geschiedschrijving', *Tijdschrift voor Genderstudies* (2003), pp. 6-15.

Van Dijk, S., '"Les jugements universellement portés sur les femmes..." Schrijfsters en lezeressen in een internationale database', *Historica*, 24 (3) (2001), pp. 3-5.

Van Heck, P., 'Ciò che poeta la lingua nostra. One Hundred and More Years of Dante Translations into Dutch', in: De Rooy, R., ed., *Divine Comedies for the New Millenium. Recent Dante Translations in America and the Netherlands* (Amsterdam, 2003), pp. 75-128.

Van Voorst, S., 'Wordt vervolgd: de receptie van Nederlandse migrantenliteratuur', *Neerlandica extra muros* 45 (1) (2007), pp. 11-22.

Venuti, L., *The Translator's Invisibility. A History of Translation* (London/New York, 2008).

Venuti, L., *The Translator's Invisibility. A History of Translation* (London/New York, 1995).

Verbeke, M., *Rijksmiddelbaar onderwijs voor meisjes: 100 jaar geleden een werkelijkheid* (Ghent, 1982).

Verboven, K., Carlier, M. and Dumulyn, J., 'A Short Manual to the Art of Prosopography', in: Keats-Rohan, K.S.B., ed., *Prosopography Approaches and Applications. A Handbook* (Oxford, 2007).

Vermeylen, A., 'Vlaamsche en Europeesche Beweging', *Van Nu en Straks* II (4) (1900), pp. 299-310.

Vervliet, R., Keunen, B. and Codde, Ph., eds., *Literatuur als woord en daad: opstellen over tekst en context in de late 19e eeuw* (Brussels, 2000).

Vinka, M. and Scheller, E., 'The Saami Languages', in: *The Barents Encyclopedia* (forthcoming).

Von Flotow, L., *Translation and Gender. Translating in the 'Era of Feminism'* (Manchester/Ottowa, 1997).

Wallace, A.F.C., 'Revitalization Movements', *American Anthropologist, New Series* 58 (2) (1956), pp. 264-281.

Warnqvist, Å., *Poesifloden: utgivningen av diktsamlingar i Sverige 1976-1995* (Uppsala, 2007).

Wendelius, L., *Den dubbla identiteten. Immigrant- och minoritetslitteratur på svenska 1970-2000* (Uppsala, 2002).

Wikén Bonde, I., 'Van het ene polysysteem naar het andere. De receptie van de Vijftigers in het Zweedse literaire veld', in: Broomans, P. et al., eds., *Object: Nederlandse literatuur in het buitenland. Methode: onbekend. Vormen van onderzoek naar de receptie van literatuur uit het Nederlandse taalgebied* (Groningen, 2006), pp. 125-150.

Wilfert, B., 'Cosmopolis et l'homme invisible. Les importateurs de littérature étrangère en France, 1885-1914', *Actes de la recherche en sciences sociales* 144 (2002), pp. 33-46.

Williams, A., *Stjärnor utan stjärnbilder. Kvinnor och kanon i litteraturhistoriska översiktsverk under 1900-talet* (Uppsala, 1997).

Witt, S., 'Between the Lines: Totalitarianism and Translation in the USSR', in: Baer, B.J., ed., *Contexts, Subtexts, and Pretexts: Literary Translation in Eastern Europe and Russia* (Amsterdam/Philadelphia, 2011), pp. 149–170.

Wolf, M., 'Naar een sociologie van het vertalen', in: Naaijkens, T. et al., eds., *Denken over vertalen. Tekstboek vertaalwetenschap* (Nijmegen, 2004), pp. 389-404.

Wollin, L., 'Imperialism och xenofobi – eller ett öppet system. Kring ett brytningsskede i den svenska översättningens språkhistoria', at the IASS conference 'Översättning – adaption, interpretation, transformation' (Lund, 2010), http://www.larswollin.se.

Wouters, P., *The Citation Culture* (Amsterdam, 1999).

Websites

http://download2.hermes.asb.dk/archive/2009/Hermes42.html

http://groniek.eldoc.ub.rug.nl/FILES/root/1996/IV_96/tijalsculfac_4/article.pdf

http://kulturstorm.se/barnbok/Davvisamegiella/noraspulka_davvisamegiella.html

http://litguide.press.jhu.edu

http://nile.lub.lu.se/ojs/index.php/IASS2010

http://projekt.ht.lu.se/brefs
http://skandinaviska-oversattningar.net
http://sverigesradio.se/sida/artikel.aspx?programid=2327&artikel=3365060
http://sverigesradio.se/sida/default.aspx?programid=3124
http://sverigesradio.se/sida/gruppsida.aspx?programid=3967&grupp=13550
http://web.abo.fi/fak/hf/sve/filis
http://web.archive.org/web/20080622211621/http://www.animated-news.com/archives/00001550.html
http://www.eurozine.com/articles/2006-08-03-kongslien-en.html
http://www.homogeschiedenis.nl/thema/?onm3_catId=26
http://www.ihlia.nl/dutch/algemeen/Tijdbalk
http://www.ihlia.nl/dutch/zoeken_catalogi/tijdschrift
http://www.ihlia.nl/english/english
http://www.larswollin.se
http://www.nias.knaw.nl/Content/NIAS/Publicaties/KB%20Lectures/KBLect1.pdf
http://www.oversattarlexikon.se/
http://www.rfsl.se/?p=413
http://www.soctat.org/
http://www.storiesofconneriver.ca/EN/about/index.php
http://www.tau.ac.il/~itamarez/works/books/ez-pss1990.pdf
http://www.tinet.cat/~apym/on-line/translation/rates/rates.html
http://www.unesco.org/culture/languages-atlas/
http://www.unesco.org/new/en/culture/themes/endangered-languages/
http://www.ur.se/cugu/
http://www.ur.se/gulahalan/
http://www.ur.se/Produkter/134158-Sagor-fran-Sameland?q=samiska
http://www.ur.se/Produkter/162789-Smasagor-sydsamiska?q=sydsamiska
http://www.ur.se/Produkter/162789-Smasagor-sydsamiska?q=sydsamiska
http://www.ur.se/samasta/
http://www.womenwriters.nl/

Index

About the Studies on Cultural Transfer and Transmission series

The Studies on Cultural Transfer and Transmission series (CTaT) deals with 'cultural transfer', defined as the one-way activity of translating a literary text, for example, and 'cultural transmission', considered as the reciprocal activity of sharing cultural and literary information. The research themes include gender, minorities, cultural transfer and transmission history.

Volumes in the series:

From Darwin to Weil
Women as Transmitters of Ideas
Petra Broomans (ed.)

In the Vanguard of Cultural Transfer
Cultural Transmitters and Authors in Peripheral Literary Fields
Petra Broomans and Marta Ronne (eds.)

The Invasion of Books in Peripheral Literary Fields
Transmitting Preferences and Images in Media, Networks and Translation
Petra Broomans and Ester Jiresch (eds.)

Rethinking Cultural Transfer and Transmission
Reflections and New Perspectives
Petra Broomans and Sandra van Voorst (eds.),
Karina Smits (assistant ed.)

Forthcoming:

Battles and Borders
Perspectives on Cultural Transmission and Literature in Minor Language Areas
Edited by Petra Broomans (chief editor), Roald van Elswijk, Goffe Jensma, Ester Jiresch, Janke Klok

Zweedse literatuur in Nederland en Vlaanderen (1491-2007), een bibliografie (Swedish literature in the Netherlands and Flanders (1491-2007), a bibliography)
Compiled and edited by Petra Broomans and Ingeborg Kroon

Noorse auteurs in Nederlandse vertaling
Een bibliografie over de periode 1741-2012
Compiled by Raf de Saeger

9 789491 431197
13W75647/ T1/ 9789491431197